LEADERSHIP THEORY

&

SOCIAL CHANGE

Formal and Informal Aspects of
Leadership in Organizations

PARATAN BALLOO, MBA, DPHIL

GlobalEdAdvance
Press

Leadership Theory & Social Change

Formal and Informal Aspects of Leadership in Organizations

Copyright © 2016, 2018 by Paratan Balloo

Library of Congress Control Number: 2016935470

Balloo, Paratan 1957 —

   Leadership Theory & Social Change

   ISBN 978-1-935434-79-5 Print

   ISBN 978-1-935434-95-5 eBook

Subject Codes and Description: 1. EDU032000 Education: Leadership 2. BUS071000 Business and Economics: Leadership 3. EDU036000 Education: Organizations and Institutions

   Cover design by Barton Green

   Printed in Australia, Brazil, France, Germany, Italy, Poland, Spain, UK, and USA Also available on Espresso Book Machine.

   Order books from www.gea-books.com/bookstore/ or any place good books are sold.

Published by

GlobalEdAdvance Press

a division of

Global Educational Advance, Inc.

www.gea-books.com

Contents

Publisher's Preface

The Need for Selfless Leadership

The faith-based community has failed to shape leaders to advance positive social change. It seems that most individuals, given the opportunity to lead, become followers rather than leaders. Why does this happen? Such individuals are prone to asked themselves, "What do the people want?" rather than "What is best for the Kingdom of God?" The nature of discipleship usually develops persons eager to follow the guidance of Christ in each endeavor of life. This is not bad, but many disciples fail to develop the aggressive mindset required to lead. A teachable spirit is considered meekness; however, meekness may easily become weakness in the eyes of others.

In fact, Peter, the future leader of Christianity, displayed forceful behavior when he drew his sword in defense of Jesus in the garden. Such action cost the High Priest's servant an ear, but demonstrated that Peter had not lost his aggressiveness in defense of Cause. Although it was part of God's Master Plan for Jesus to be taken, condemned, and crucified, Jesus had clearly taught the Disciples that His Mission was not to bring peace but division. According to Matthew 10 the separation would be based on an individual's personal acceptance or rejection of Christ. Obviously, from the garden experience and other hard lessons, Peter learned to focus his aggression and become a leader in the pristine church. Leaders are not born; they are forged in the harshness of real life experience. Leadership is developed in the choices of a way forward in the midst of difficulty.

What are the distinctive attributes possessed by individuals who develop the aptitude to lead others toward positive change? Retired Gen. Tommy Franks, besides being a decorated soldier and recognized leader of aggressive forces, he traveled the world, speaking on leadership, character and the value of social equality. His identification of the essential elements of leadership came out of years of observation of individuals engaged in aggressive action in world affairs.

Gen. Franks learned that the relationship between soldiers and leaders was premised on a foundation of trust and that the trust factor was so deeply embedded that even the possibility of death could not break it. Out of this reasoning, he developed the Four Stars of Leadership: character, communication, common vision and caring. According to his career experience and evaluation he determined the essential elements of leadership.

- Character was the distinctive quality utilized to fully release their values, ethics and morals.

- Communication was a leadership act by which information was exchanged to focus others on the objective.

- Common vision was the ability to enable a group to see beyond the present to the long-range objective and how to get there.

- Caring was the ability to truly care for others and act on behalf of, and in the best interest of others. This is selfless leadership.

The consequences of weak leadership are devastating to the faith-based community. The need is for selfless leaders who will act quickly, but thoughtfully at each opportunity to move the moral and ethical cause of Christianity forward. Such action will bring positive social change to individuals, families, congregations, and faith-based groups and ultimately to the communities they serve. Jesus was aggressive! He clearly said, "As the Father sent me into the world, so send I you!" (John 20:21)

—Hollis L. Green, ThD, PhD

Leadership is...

- a **process**...
- that involves **influence**,
- that is carried out in a **group** context,
- and that aims to achieve a **common goal**.

Experience of leadership

in role

self as Leader

Action planning
to change

Reflection on
experiences

Leader
behaviour

Self as
leader

Self

Role

of self as leader

of leadership

Theories of leadership

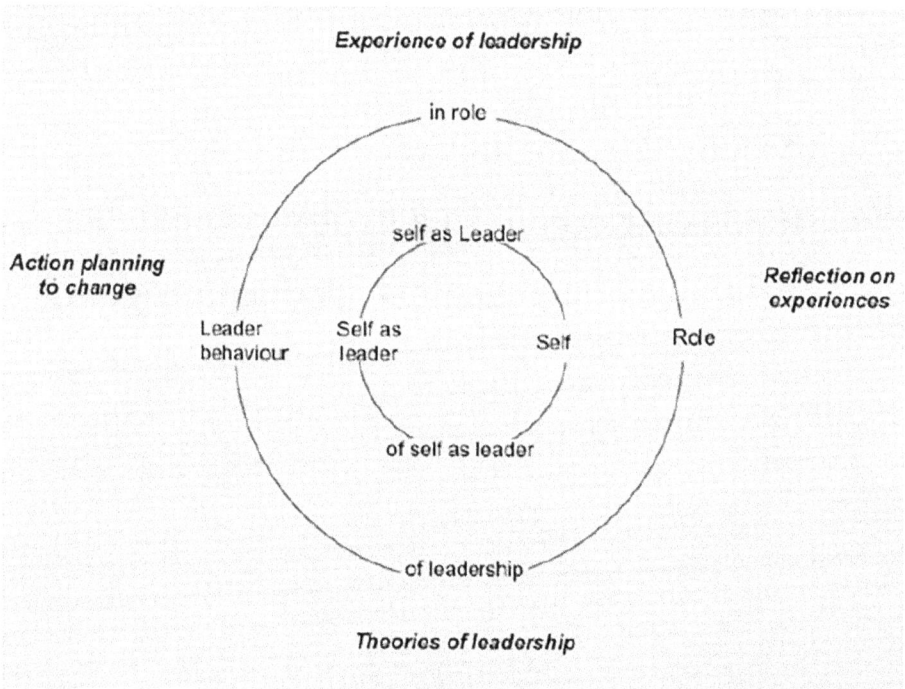

Figure 1.1 The leadership learning cycle

1

Learning About Leadership

Learning Objectives:

- Understand and work with the circles of leader development;
- Acknowledge that leading is about change;
- Understand the structure of the book and how it relates to the circles of leadership development.

This book considers the formal and informal aspects of leadership in organizations. Major theories of leadership will be discussed and investigated for application into the structure, processes, and behavior of organized groups. The sympathetic and cybernetic aspects of leadership are considered in the context of process of social change.

The author examines Social Change globally from both macro and micro perspectives; both long and short term. There are several dimensions including individual change, institutional change, social movements, and nonviolence, and eternal change.

See **Figure 1.1** on page opposite: The **outer circle** is based upon acknowledging your experience of leadership in organizations, reflecting upon that experience, examining those experiences and reflections against the theories of leadership and then planning how you might plan to change your own leadership and leadership in your organization.

The **inner circle** is about you. Beginning with your personal experience of being a leader, reflecting upon that experience, examining those reflections against theories of persons as leaders, and then planning to change and develop yourself as a leader.

Social theories are theoretical frameworks which are used to study and interpret social phenomena within a particular school of thought. An essential tool used by social scientists, theories relate to historical debates over the most valid and reliable methodologies (e.g. positivism and anti-positivism), as well as the primacy of either structure or agency. Certain social theories attempt to remain strictly scientific, descriptive, and objective. Conflict theories, by contrast, present ostensibly normative positions, and often critique the ideological aspects inherent in conventional, traditional thought.

Warren Bennis, a noted writer on leadership, borrowed William Shakespeare's idea of the seven stages of a man's life to consider the parallel stages of a leader's development:

The infant	executive in need of a mentor	The young graduate
The schoolboy	must learn and then act in public, still in need of mentors	The unit leader
The lover	wonders anxiously about his success and his attachment to the career and organisation	The group leader
The bearded soldier	is now a leader of substance who must be willing to accept people better than himself as talented staff.	The divisional leader
The general	must be open to the truth, listen and hear what people say to him	The strategic leader
The statesman	works at wisdom for the organisation, is a policy-maker	The policy leader
The sage	embraces the role of mentor	The senior non-executive director

Three types of leadership:

1. **Traditional**, by which he meant that the leader's authority came from social, political and institutional continuity. Examples are kings, tribal leaders, religious leaders and such.

2. **Rational legal**, where the leader's authority came from constitutions of nations and organizations. Examples are presidents, prime ministers, trade union officers etc.

3. **Charismatic**, where the leader's authority came from inside the person and was accepted by those who were inspired to follow.

- **Accidental leadership** will not focus upon any dynamic of change but may, like a stopped clock, find a correct solution with the passage of time.

- **Preservative leadership** will seek to keep the traditions and business practices intact, perhaps with considerable attention to both the effectiveness of those practices and the efficiency of the business processes.

- **Enabling leadership** will work to allow others, probably more junior but not necessarily so, to use their own leadership in their work.

- **Strategic leadership** will be concerned with purpose and their achievement in the evolving context in which the business seeks to operate.

Table 1.1   Leadership and Orientation to Change

Leadership Group		
	Modes of working	
Change orientation is	*Low Interventionist*	*High Interventionist*
Towards no change	Accidental: Que sera sera	Preservative: maintaining
Towards change	Enabling: encouraging	Strategic: directive

The **normative culture** is where all thought and action is infused with attention to and debates about values, and people belong because they subscribe to the values. The **instrumental cultures** are those where people belong because they can get something they want and are prepared to compromise in order to get it; business organizations have much of this characteristic. **Coercive** organizations require and force people to belong: prisons and armies are such.

Top leaders, it appears, tend to be very careful to listen to a range of views and relatively slow to come to a view. It seems that judgment is more important for them as it forms the context within which decisions can be made. Here is a glimpse of the difference between policy and strategy. Policy is of the whole society, of the whole community, and shapes the values, beliefs and assumptions of the organization.

2

Trait Theory of Leadership

Learning Objectives

- State the underlying premise of trait theory in the study of leadership;
- Identify the early methods employed to identify leadership traits;
- List the major reasons why trait theory is an attractive approach to studying successful leadership;
- Describe the advantages and shortcomings of identifying traits through the biographies of great leaders;
- Discuss the advantages and shortcomings of identifying traits through the study of leaders' physical characteristics;
- Demonstrate the advantages and shortcomings of identifying traits through psychometric testing;
- Explain the correlation between intelligence and leadership success;
- Explain the correlation between emotional intelligence and leadership success;
- Describe how the perspective of important leadership traits may be affected by culture;
- List the most commonly identified leadership traits from the research.

Trait theories:

- **Leadership** – influencing the attitudes, beliefs. behaviors and feeling of people.

- **Trait theory** – also great man focus on leader

- **Methods** – Biographical Analysis, physical characteristics, psychological, external perceptions.

- **Testing** – Physical measurements, psychometric tests, physical traits, personality characteristics.

- **Traits from followers' perspective** – Honest, forward looking, inspiring, competent, fair minded, supportive, broadminded, intelligent

- **Psychological workplace needs of successful leaders** – achievement, power, affiliation

- **Cognitive** (winning minds) and **EI** (wining hearts)

- **Most common leadership traits** – physical attractiveness, intelligence, confidence, social skills, integrity, (most essential), desire to lead (essential) PICSID

Interviews with/by Charles Handy

Core-periphery theory is based on the notion that as one region or state expands in economic prosperity; it must engulf regions nearby to ensure ongoing economic and political success. The area of high growth or former high growth becomes known as the core, and the neighboring area is the periphery. Cores and peripheries can be towns, cities, states, or nations. Trees and planets have cores, and some day in the future it is likely that entire planets could be considered as cores, semi-peripheries, or peripheries under world-systems theory.

Core expansion trends and methods

On a *simplified* scale, when a city grows in popularity, it must expand its borders to continue to supply the population with the standard of living they are used to (eg variety of products, standard of living, etc). Traditionally, the inner city core will first expand to areas of geographic similarity; for instance, a neighboring town may find itself becoming a suburb of the city.

When geographic peripheries become exhausted (either because resources have dried up or the economies of scale have balanced out), the core then seeks out peripheries that are culturally similar and share the same language as the core. Only when the core has exhausted all advantageous options of geographic and cultural similarity will it seek to expand to a periphery that is truly foreign. This is because a foreign periphery carries a high risk of not complying with requests from the core.

An example of traditional core-periphery theory exhausting regional options and adopting an international scale can be found in the European colonization of Africa. Core nations, such as England, Germany and France, sought to extract resources in the face of cultural disparity.

Because these cultural differences were perceived as vast, military presence was necessary to ensure the expansion of these cores into Africa.

Whereas peripheries bearing geographic or cultural similarity to the core can often benefit in the long run, through what is known as trickle-down economics, peripheries that have vast cultural differences often lack negotiation rights in their colonisation. When this happens, trickle-up economics apply, and peripheries watch as their resources drain away towards the core. The more a periphery becomes colonised, the less it is able to resist the core. The probability of civil or transnational war then starts to slowly approach 1 (certainty).

Semi-periphery

Many experts contest that the core-periphery system is far too simple and hold that there is an additional aspect to society that has been markedly left out. They maintain that the semi-periphery is also an important middle ground between the core and the periphery. This is an area that is more self sufficient and developed than the periphery, but not to the extent of the core. Immanuel Wallerstein argues that the semi-periphery is important because it bridges the gap between the rich core countries and the poor periphery countries. It provides balance and order keeping the world from political and economic crisis in same way that the middle class does on the national level in stable core countries.

Dealing with inequality

Answers to the disparity between cores and peripheries are most complex on the international level. Some speculation holds that free trade is the answer because it could allow for periphery countries to concentrate on producing goods for which they have an aptitude. Nonetheless, critics of this claim still maintain that it would make little difference because the established core countries would still dominate.

On the urban level, responding to the inequality between core areas and periphery areas is also difficult, but not impossible. The key is to bring back to life the vitality of struggling neighborhoods and reestablish them as complements to the city. It takes knowledgeable foresight by city officials as well as action through the entire community to accomplish this. Each situation may require a different course of action whether it is a radical change or only a slight nudge in the right direction.

Since areas overlap or include each other and all have a middle and an edge, cores and peripheries are everywhere and on every level. Galaxies have a galactic core; vertebrates have a peripheral nervous system; communication systems have a core network; oceans have a shoreline and so forth. Growth and development in one area is going to have a counter affect in an adjacent area to some degree. This backlash effect causes an inequality between different areas and amongst the people who live in each area.

Trait Theory of Leadership

*From OB. ...**Trait approach to leadership** - Leader traits are referred to personal characteristics (physical, social background, intellectual, personality, work orientation, interpersonal skills). Other traits – **logical thinking** (putting ides into simpler forms, persuading others, explaining things in unique ways) **persistence** (treating setbacks as small mistakes, working long hours, trying to succeed against odds) **empowerment** (getting people excited about goals, being energetic and enthusiastic, making subordinates believe they can achieve excellence) **Self-Control** (working under heavy pressure, remaining even-tempered, resisting intimidation). **Weakness of Trait approach** – failure to take into account the situation in which leadership occurs. Leadership is an influence process and can not occur the context of interpersonal relations. Leader traits are related to who gets promoted than who is an effective leader.*

Leadership Book: Leadership: theme – involves influencing the attitudes, beliefs, behaviours, and feelings of other people.

Trait Theory – Also called" Great man" 1930 – 40's was the first approach discussed.

- Focuses exclusively on the leader not the situation or the followers therefore more straight forward.

- Concerned with what traits are important and who possesses these traits

- Theory argues that it is the leader and his personality and other char. That are central to leadership

- Concerned with uncovering the particular characteristics that differentiated leaders from non leaders to find what captured the admiration of other people.

- Leaders are born with special characteristics rather than made

- org can develop methods to identify leaders and find ways to develop and enhance traits in others

- Also considered to be a source of personal awareness – assess own traits

Methods of identifying leadership traits

Biographical analysis	Analyzing the traits of historical heroes, interviews with successful leaders
	Problems with this approach:
	1. Most individual selected are historical which limits the analysis to historical information.
	2. Traits identified are the ones author would consider to be important for a leader and may overlook other obvious traits.
	3. Transferability – would these traits have relevance in today's society?
Physical characteristics	Correlating with height, weight, voice. Analyzing skull shape, brain structure and neurological make up.
Psychological characteristics	Correlating leadership with level of personality traits – extroversion, dominance, self reliance, level of intelligence, level of emotional intelligence.
External perceptions	Identifying leadership traits valued by followers and particular cultures.

Testing for traits:

1. Physical measurements – head size – feeling bumps on heads, Also use graphology and handwriting to assess personality

2. Psychometric tests – can be administered to large #of people, validated and assessed for validity. Often test on a bipolar scale. Big 5 traits – open-mindedness, conscientiousness, agreeableness, emotional stability and extroversion. Key issue is how to define a trait and then devising an appropriate method to measure it. The tests have not been able to help establish a profile of psychological traits with highly successful leaders but it does tell us that possessing certain traits and characteristics are an advantage for leaders.

3. Physical traits: argued that physical characteristics alone are insufficient to explain why some people become leaders; persuasive communication does seem to be influenced by the image and the perceived credibility of those delivering the message. Physical char may help but do not guarantee success.

4. Personality characteristics: Intelligence and leadership- studies find that leaders tend to be more intelligent, dominant, self-confident and knowledgeable of the task than non-leaders. Extremely high IQ scores are not associated with effective leadership – leaders are intelligent but not too much.

Summary of specific traits for leadership success

Stodgill	Mann	Stodgill
1948	1956	1974
Intelligence	Dominance	Sociability
Alertness	Masculinity	Tolerance
Sociability	Adjustment	Responsibility
Persistence	Intelligence	Initiative
Insight	Conservatism	Persistence
Self-	extroversion	Achievement
confidence		Insight
Initiative		Self-confidence
		Cooperativeness
		Influence
Lord	Kirkpatrick	Hogan
1986	and Locke 1991	1994
Intelligence	Drive	Extroversion
	Motivation	Energy
Masculinity	Integrity	Agreeableness
dominance	confidence	conscientiousness
	cognitive ability	
	task knowledge	

Traits from the follower's perspective: What do you look for in a leader? Honest, forward looking, inspiring, competent, fair minded, supportive, broadminded, intelligent. Effective leadership does not necessarily equate with "good" (ethical) outcomes and that leadership can have dark sides.

Personality traits of successful business leaders: Cooper and Highley (1985)

1. Loner attitude and a sense of marginalization

2. Motivation and drive leading to abundance of energy and stamina

3. Deep-seated belief system – strong sense of mission or cause

4. Early responsibility

5. Personal charisma

6. Well developed people skills ability to communicate and to be open and honest

7. A childhood that involved insecurity and loss

Dulewicz and Herbert identified high flyers scored highly on the following dimensions: Assertiveness, Risk taking, Achievement, Motivation, Competitiveness

Psychological workplace needs of successful leaders: psychological needs are considered to be a powerful motivator of human behaviour. Three most important:

- **Need for achievement** – desire to overcome obstacles and strive to do something difficult, quickly and well. Less effective because they put their own success first

- **Need for Power** – desire for control and influence.

- **Need for affiliation** – desire to form good relationships and sense of belonging. Causes the leader to put their popularity first.

Social and emotional intelligence: Many leadership descriptions emphasize that leadership is about winning the minds and hearts of other. Winning minds is an intellectual task and requires application of cognitive skills (reasoning, logic). Winning hearts is an emotional task and requires exercise of social and emotional intelligence. Goleman suggests that EI is more predictive of leadership achievement, life success, and general well being than cognitive intelligence (IQ).

EI is demonstrated by: Self awareness of one's own emotions – Leaders confident and know what motivates them. Aware of situations that cause them to be negative. Easily recognise when they are sad, happy, angry or frightened.

Self management- feelings are able to control anger and disruptive emotions while maintaining their integrity. Do not become overwhelmed by negative emotions.

Awareness of others- sensitive to others and recognised their efforts and contribution. Know when to speak when to stay silent.

Pursing the goal- able to achieve high standards, high level initiative even in the face of adversity

Relationship with others- ability to influence others in non-threatening way and do not avoid dealing with feelings

Culture and leadership Traits: Leadership categorization theory believes that the better the match between the leadership concepts held by followers and the leader's display of those attributes, the more likely the followers will see the leader as a leader.

Most commonly Identified Leadership traits: Physical attractiveness, (Imp to remember that physical presentation can easily fade away if lacking in other leadership traits.) **Intelligence, Confidence, Social Skills, Integrity** (most essential), **the desire to lead** (essential trait).

Table 2.4 **Attributes and drawbacks of principal leadership traits**

Traits	Main attributes	Main drawbacks
Heroic	• Is intuitively appealing • Identifies the characteristics of successful leaders from many different times and settings	• Heroes, generals and politicians, may have limited relevance to today's business leaders • Traits contributing to success are the opinions of biographers
Physical	• Relatively easy to assess • Research shows that height and attractiveness are an asset to leaders, at least initially	• Are numerous examples of outstanding leaders who lack such traits
Personality	• A huge number of psychometric tests and research are available • Provide a substantial amount of feedback to the individual • Characteristics such as extroversion and self-confidence correlate with leadership effectiveness	• Play a supporting role in selection since personality traits are only moderately predictive of leadership success • Traits may not be readily developed if lacking

Intelligence (IQ)	• Is a moderate correlation between intelligence and leadership success • IQ is a common measurement, readily understood	• Too much intelligence interferes with successful leadership • Intelligence is relatively fixed, not readily susceptible to development • Intelligence alone is not enough: the leader must also understand the context and have other skills
Emotional Intelligence (EI)	• Initial research suggests EI is more predictive of leadership than IQ • Appeals due to its focus on managing emotions and interrelating with others • May be developed through training	• Has been popularised, but EI traits may not be significantly different from previously identified personality traits such as sociability, introspection and self-confidence.
Follower Preferences	• Has face validity from those who choose to follow the leaders • Identifies traits not found in psychometric tests such as honesty, consideration and being competent	• Little research available to correlate follower chosen traits with actual success • Follower preferences may be influenced by the leader's level of popularity

Learning Summary: Chapter 2

- Trait theory attempts to understand leadership effectiveness through the identification of personal characteristics such as personality, body shape or intelligence which correlate positively with successful leadership.

- Trait theory is an attractive way for organizations to study leadership. If the traits that successful leaders possess can be identified, then those traits can be used to identify future leaders.

- An initial approach to trait research was through examining the biographies of great, even heroic, leaders. However, the practical application of such studies has been limited.

- Physical assessment of leaders is a second approach. Although some approaches such as measuring head shape, brain structure and so on have been largely discredited, there does appear to be some correlation between leadership effectiveness and the individual's physical makeup. For example, height appears to be an advantage.

- Psychometric testing has been used to identify the relationship between leadership success and a variety of psychological characteristics such as intelligence, personality traits, psychological needs and emotional intelligence.

- When followers are asked which traits are required in effective leaders, they tend to identify traits such as honesty, being forward-looking, being inspiring, and being competent and fair-minded. Such traits are not commonly assessed through psychometric tests.

- A leader who exhibits the traits of a successful leader may not, however, necessarily be an ethical leader (*see* Chapter 7)

- Traits valued in leaders are often somewhat different from culture to culture (*see* Chapter 5).

- Although psychometric testing is commonly used to test for leadership traits, it largely fulfils a supporting role in the selection of leaders as its predictive qualities appear to be quite limited.

- Traits commonly found to correlate with successful leadership from across a variety of studies include physical attractiveness, intelligence, confidence, social skills, integrity and the desire to lead.

3

Behaviour Theory of Leadership

Learning Objectives

- Describe the difference between the trait theory of leadership and the behavior theory of leadership;
- List the two major dimensions of early leadership theories as focus on task and focus on relationship;
- Identify the difference between mcgregor's theory x manager and the theory y manager;
- List the different styles of management proposed by blake and mouton in their managerial grid;
- Describe the underlying premise of contingency theory;
- Describe the diagnostic process used in hersey and blanchard's situational leadership model;
- List and describe the four situational leadership styles of the model;
- State the concepts behind fiedler's contingency model;
- State the concepts underpinning path–goal theory.

Behavioral theory – What the leader does rather than traits. Theory holds that leaders are made, not born.

Hawthorne Effect. – Study of women production works at GE. Reason for the productivity was that the women were receiving extra attention and were seen as having status within the workforce: in essence, they felt special.

Autocratic – Strong direction. **Democratic** (receive considerable support, advice and encouragement from leader). **Laissez-faire** (given no task guidance and interacted minimally with the leader).

From the Lewin study - effective leadership had two distinct dimensions – the ability to accomplish a given task and the ability to develop motivating and satisfying relationships with those one leads. From Lewin's work, one can easily come to the conclusion that a democratic leadership style is best.

Leadership theories:

Douglas McGregor - The **Theory X** direct work and closely monitor the workforce, because people tend to be lazy by nature, lack ambition, prefer to let others be responsible, and resist change. Theory X manager would be 'hard' or 'strong', keeping tight control. **Theory Y** holds that if employees have become passive and resistant, it is because of their experience in organisations. Management's role is to arrange the working environment and methods of operations so that people feel trusted, take on responsibility, and achieve their personal goals by directing their efforts toward achieving organisational goals.

Blake and Mouton's Managerial Grid (two factor leadership grid) They propose that there are five important positions on the grid to consider.

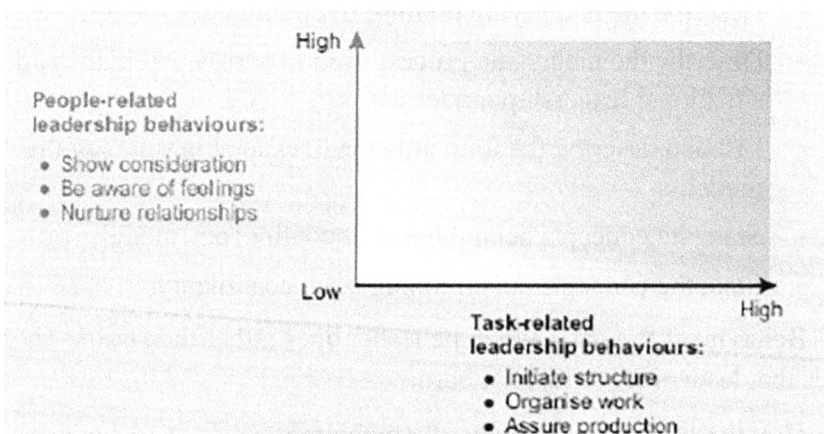

People-related leadership behaviours:

- Show consideration
- Be aware of feelings
- Nurture relationships

Task-related leadership behaviours:

- Initiate structure
- Organise work
- Assure production

Figure 3.1

Impoverished management

- Low on consideration and low on initiating structure

- Nondirective and nonparticipative

- Uninspiring and ineffective leadership

Country club management

- High on consideration and low on initiating structure

- Highly participative but nondirective

- Individuals might find working with such a leader to be a pleasant and undemanding experience at a personal level but lacking in challenge and stimulation. The leader may be well liked but ineffectual.

Organisation (wo)man

- A middle of the road style of leadership associated with promoting moderate rather than high performance

- Leader tries to balance the contradiction between production and the needs of individuals

- Lack of strong direction often leads to team complacency and lack of challenge.

Authority–obedience

- Low on consideration and high on initiating structure

- Highly task directive

- Leader maintains close supervision and control over team members

- Promotes compliance rather than task commitment or high levels of involvement.

Team management

- Both high on consideration and high on initiating structure

- Promotes high levels of task commitment and relationships based on trust and respect

- The 'best' style of management to which leaders should aspire

Contingency Theories of leadership: An influential theory of situational leadership is that proposed by Tannenbaum and Schmidt

(1973); it conceptualizes leadership behaviour along a continuum dependent upon the degree to which leaders use their authority. Tannenbaum and Schmidt do not advocate one 'best way' of leadership, but rather emphasize the need for leader flexibility. The four styles may be summarized as follows:

- **Tells.** This is an authoritarian style. The role of those they lead is simply to follow these instructions. This style is based on the assumption that followers have no useful role to play in decision making, possibly because of lack of ability, knowledge or motivation.

- **Sells.** A 'selling' style is little different from a 'telling' style, except that instructions and directions are articulated in a softer and more persuasive way. Leaders still take control and make decisions. The use of persuasion represents an attempt to try and secure willing compliance rather than simply impose the decision.

- **Consults.** Leaders consult with followers and obtain their views. These views are taken into account, but leaders reserve the right to make the final decision, which may or may not be in line with the views of others.

- **Joins.** This is a totally participative style. Leaders join with followers to make a decision in which all views are represented.

Situational Leadership: A very popular development of the contingency approach to leadership is Hersey and Blanchard's (1988) model of situational leadership, which rests on similar basic assumptions

- There is no single all purpose leadership style, but rather what is appropriate depends upon the nature of the follower(s) and the demands and requirements of the task.

- The leader's behaviour has two independent components: directive behaviour and supportive behaviour. **Directive behavior** relates to the extent to which the leader provides structure and guidance concerning the task. **Supportive behaviour** relates to the extent to which the leader supports and acts with consideration towards followers.

The model emphasizes four leadership styles dependent upon one major situational factor, the **developmental level** of the follower for any given task.(three factors: having the technical knowledge, skills or competence to execute the task; the level of commitment to pursue the task; and the level of confidence that he or she will be successful at the task.)

The four leadership styles that are to be matched with the respective follower development levels are:

- **S1 Telling (or directing).** the follower is judged to need clear direction.
- **S2 Selling (or coaching).** follower's requires both direction and support.
- **S3 Participating (or supporting).** follower is considered to have adequate mastery of the skills required for the job, but some support is required.
- **S4 Delegating.** This follower will have mastered the task, has confidence, and so requires only that the task be delegated with little requirement for supervision.

Table 3.1 Diagnosing the follower's development level

Development level				
Diagnostic factors	*D-4* *peak performer*	*D-3* *regular contributor*	*D-2 disillutioned learner*	*D-1* *enthusiastic beginner*
Competence on *this* task	**Master** Has mastered the task	**Sufficient** Can normally do the task	**Marginal** Cannot do the entire task adequately	**Low** Can do little if any of the task
Commitment to *this* task	**High** Wants to do the task perfectly	**Varies** Commitment to the task varies	**Low to variable** Commitment to the task varies	**High to low** Varies from motivated to lacking committment
Confidence on *this* task	**High** Confident about doing the task	**Varies** between confidence and insecurity	**Varies insecure** Insecure about doing the task	**Low** Insecure about doing the task

Source: Adapted from Hersey and Blanchard

Table 3.2 A contingency model of leadership

Leader member relations	Good				Poor			
Task structure	High		Low		High		Low	
Position Power	Strong	Weak	Strong	Weak	Strong	Weak	Strong	Weak
Preferred leadership style (LPC score)	1 2 3 • Low relationship motivated • Moderate relationship motivated		4 5 6 • High relationship motivated		7 8 • Low relationship motivated			

Fielder's contingency model: Fiedler developed a measure called the **least preferred coworker** (LPC) scale. Leaders who attain a high LPC score are considered to have high self-esteem needs and so derive considerable satisfaction from interpersonal relationships. They will expend a lot of energy in providing support and consideration to improve relationships in situations where relationships are poor. In contrast, leaders with low LPC scores are considered to have high task accomplishment needs and so derive considerable satisfaction from task performance and achieving objectives. their primary motivation will be to focus on task accomplishment. theory suggests that effective leadership behaviour is dependent upon both the favourability of the situation and the degree of situational control. Rather the situation itself should be changed to fit the leader, or the leader should be assigned to situations that best fit his or her style.

- **Leader member relations** (good/poor): The degree to which a leader is trusted and liked by group members, and their willingness to support the leader and follow his/her guidance, the group atmosphere.

- **Task structure** (high/low): The extent to which the task is clearly defined for the group, and the extent to which it can be carried out by detailed instructions or standard procedures. Highly structured tasks give the leader more control, whereas nebulous tasks diminish the leader's control.

- **Position power**: The amount of power and influence the leader has in the organization, including the ability to give out rewards and punishments. If the leader can hire and fire, he or she has considerable position power.

PATH GOAL Theory

It is influenced by theories of motivation, particularly what is termed **expectancy– valence theory.** The path–goal theory of leadership maintains that a leader should exercise the style of leadership that is most effective in influencing employees' perceptions of the goals they need to achieve and the path (or way) in which they should be achieved. This is, in contrast to the situational approach, which indicates that the leader should adapt to the development level of the follower, as well as to the contingency approach, which emphasizes matching the leadership style with situational variables.

House identified four main types of leadership behaviour:

- **directive** – giving clear instructions as to what the goal is and the way they should go about accomplishing it;

- **supportive** – encouraging and supporting individuals in accomplishing the goal;

- **participative** – involving individuals in the goal setting process, and listening to their opinions and views;

- **achievement oriented** – setting challenging goals, and building confidence in followers to achieve those goals.

Table 3.3　　Path-goal theory leadership styles

	Directive	Supportive	Participative	Achievement oriented
Works best when	Subordinates are dogmatic, authoritarian, prefer rules and procedures Task demands are nebulous, procedures are unclear	Subordinates require nurturing and encouragement The task is quite, structured, satisfying or causing frustration	Subordinates prefer to work autonomously, feel they have control The task requires clarification	Subordinates will take on challenges, are willing to personally develop The task lacks clarity

An advantage of Path–Goal Theory is that it is uncomplicated and relatively straightforward. Criticism of Path–Goal Theory is that it is only partially supported by research conducted to support its validity. another concern is that path–goal theory may focus too heavily on the actions of the leader at the expense of the followers. With such an approach, followers could become overly dependent on the leader at the expense of their own development.

What a leader does - leaders are not born, they are made.

Kurt Lewin	McGregor (XY)	Blake and Mourton	Tannenbaumn & Schmidt	Hersey & Blanchard	Fielder	House Path-Goal
ADL: Autocratic Democratic Laissez-faire	TR: Task Relationship	GRID: Managerial Grid	TSCJ: Tells Sells Consults Joins	TSPD: Telling Selling Participating Delegating	LPC: Least preferred coworker	DSPA: Directive Supportive Participative Achievement

Summary

Some theorists suggest that the style should be determined by the follower's development level (Situational Leadership), while other theorists submit that leadership style is probably fixed and therefore the leader should be assigned to a situation where he or she can be most successful (Contingency Theory). Yet another behaviour theory school of thought is that an analysis of the follower's goal orientation combined with the relative clarity of the task will determine the most effective leadership approach (Path–Goal Theory).

Table 3.4 Attributes and drawbacks of principal leadership behaviour theories

Theory	Main attributes	Main drawbacks
McGregor's Theory X Theory Y	• Clearly defines the two major orientations of leadership behaviours: task and relationship • Promotes the 'people factor' in leadership behaviours	• Tends to oversimplify leadership as a choice between either focusing on task or focusing on relationship
Blake and Mouton's Managerial Grid	• Develops the concept that task and relationship orientations are not mutually exclusive • Creates a measurement instrument to assess leadership style	• Promotes the concept that there is one 'best' style of leadership focusing on both task as well as relationship • No consistent research has supported the effectiveness of this approach
Situational leadership (Wright, Tannenbaum and Schmidt, Hersey and Blanchard)	• Focuses on follower needs rather than a leader's preferred style • Is conceptually attractive and easy to apply • Proposes that leadership behaviours should be contingent upon the particular situation	• Conceptual underpinnings are not clearly defined or understood • Research only partially supports the effectiveness of this approach
Fiedler's contingency model	• Advocates placing leaders in situations where they are most likely to be effective • Research indicates the model has good predictive qualities • Proposes that differing leadership styles will be effective in different situations, depending on leader–member relations, level of task structure and positional power	• The theory is not able to explain 'why' some styles work in certain situations and not in others • In practice, the model is quite cumbersome, difficult to use in practical situations • Advocates changing the assignment rather than developing the individual's style
Path–goal theory (Vroom, Porter and Lawler, House and Mitchell)	• Integrates motivational theory with leadership theory • Leaders should, therefore, choose actions suited to both the follower's needs and the needs of the work situation • Is uncomplicated and straightforward	• The effectiveness of the theory is only partially supported by research • Focuses too much on the leader, at the expense of the follower, perhaps causing the follower to become overly dependent

Learning Summary: Chapter 3

- Behavioral leadership theory contrasts with trait theory in that it studies leaders' behaviors, what they do, rather than their personal characteristics.

- Behavior theory holds that leaders are made, and therefore leadership effectiveness can be learned by developing and employing appropriate skills and behaviors.

- Early research identified two key dimensions of leadership behavior, a focus on achieving the task at hand and a focus on developing the relationship with the follower.

- Douglas McGregor (Theory X–Theory Y) developed the idea that leaders would tend to focus either on task or on relationship, but that to focus on one dimension would be at the expense of the other.

- Blake and Mouton submitted that a strong leadership focus on both the task and the relationship was the 'best' style of leadership.

- Contingency theory emerged in the 1970s and considers what kind of leadership style would be effective in what kind of situation.

- Hersey and Blanchard's situational leadership model became the most widely used model of behavioral theory, which diagnoses the follower's task development level before selecting the most appropriate leadership behaviors.

- The contingency model (Fiedler) proposed that leadership styles are relatively fixed, being effective in certain situations but less so in others. So leaders should be placed in situations where they will likely achieve success.

- Path–goal theory marries leadership theory with motivational theory so that the motivational needs of the follower are considered along with the work situation in selecting an effective leadership approach.

- Behavioral leadership theory is intuitively appealing, as most leaders will attribute much of their success to developmental experiences, and it also supports the idea that organizational time and resources should be placed against the development of its leadership capability.

$\underline{4}$

Transformation Theory of Leadership: Engaging Hearts and Minds

Learning Objectives

- Describe the differences in approach between transactional and transformational leaders;

- Describe the historic trends that challenged traditional views of leadership and promoted the development of transformational leadership theory;

- List the four elements that are a part of transformational leaders;

- Identify common methods in which transformational leadership behaviors are identified;

- Quote key research findings that describe the successful practices of executives who are considered to be transformational leaders;

- View charisma as being a key transformational leadership quality;

- List the behavioral attributes of those who exhibit charisma;

- Describe the methods that have been found to be successful in developing transformational leadership skills;

- Describe the key criticisms of transformational and charismatic leadership theory.

Transformation Theory of leadership:

In order to influence the attitudes, beliefs, and behaviors of others, a leader had to engage the emotions of those they sought to influence. Leaders could no longer rely on positional power only – new leaders had to earn their influence. Transformation leadership theory is associated with Burns (1978) and Bass (1990).

Table 4.1   Transactional vs transformational leadership

Transactional leaders	Transformational leaders
• Use contingent reward Leader contracts exchanges of rewards for effort, recognises good performance and promises reward for accomplishments.	• Are charismatic and provide a vision which instils pride, gains respect and trust.
• Practise management by exception (active) Leader watches and searches for deviations from required task behaviours and takes corrective action.	• Are inspirational and communicate high expectations of followers. They inspire individuals to make self-sacrifices and commit to difficult goals.
• Or practise management by exception (passive) Leader intervenes only if requirements are not met	• Are intellectually stimulating and get people to think and approach problems in new and different ways.
• May adopt a laissez-faire approach and abdicate responsibilities and/or avoid making decisions and generally 'hope for the best'.	• Show consideration and give followers individual attention and coaching.

Kouzes and Posner described "five practices of exemplary leadership"

1. **Model** the way

2. **Inspire** a shared vision

3. **Challenge** the process

4. **Enable** others to act

5. **Encourage** the heart

Transactional Leadership	Transformational Leadership
The traditional theories in modules 1 – 3 were described as transactional because they rely on the transactions to generate results. With transactions leaders followers comply with the demands of the task and leaders rewash the effort and compliance Approach is based on rational exchange (you do this and I will do this).	Leader appeal to the emotionality of the followers. They inspire followers to put aside and transcend their own personal interests to work for the benefit of higher-order goals, values, and principles. Engages the full person.
Works by aggregating commitment through the leader	Works by aggregating towards organizations vision, its greater purpose.
Leadership is about managing efficiency	Is truly about leadership that brings about change
	Behaviors are more effective in terms of: • increased organizational commitment of followers; • increased effort and financial performance; • increased job satisfaction; • greater trust in management; increased employee innovation, harmony and good citizenship; • Lower levels of work stress and burnout.

How to assess the above behaviors? Most sited measure is Multifactor Leadership questionnaire (MLQ) measures - individual's consideration, intellectual stimulation, charisma, inspirational motivation. Scales considered to comprise the components of transformational leadership include:

Leading and developing others

- Showing genuine concern for others, • Encouraging questioning, critical and strategic thinking
- Encouraging change

Leading the organization

- Networking, • Building a shared vision, • Creating a developmental culture

Personal qualities

- Acting with integrity, • Decisive, risk taking (public sector only – not a differentiator in private Sector), • Inspiring others, • Analytical and creative thinking, • Being entrepreneurial (private sector only)

Research findings of Transformational Leadership:

According to Bass (1990), leaders need to be capable of exercising *both* transformational and transactional leadership approaches, particularly in relation to contingent reward. Further, he suggests that transformational leaders have less difficulty in adopting a transactional style than the other way around.

4.4.1 Transformational leadership and successful executives:

Bennis and Nanus (1985) and Tichy and DeVanna (1990) used similar methodologies (open-ended questionnaires) to interview chief executives at major corporations regarding their leadership practices. They categorized and analyzed the responses to their interviews, looked for commonalities and identified four common practices or strategies employed by their study group:

1. **Vision.** These leaders created a clear, realistic, believable and attractive vision which pulled people into supporting organizational goals. Followers felt empowered as significant contributors towards that vision.

2. **Social architecture.** These leaders created a shared meaning that transformed values and culture so that employees accepted the new philosophy and direction of the organization.

3. **Trust.** Not surprisingly, these leaders were found to develop trust by setting an example, exemplifying standards of behavior. They were transparent in their beliefs, stood by their promises, and were seen to be eminently reliable, even in times of uncertainty.

4. **Positive self-regard.** Knowing their strengths and weaknesses, the leaders capitalized on their strengths rather than dwelling on their limitations. This process also appeared to have a similar impact on their followers.

4.4.2 Transformational Leadership and the management of change:

Tichy and DeVanna studied how these executives had managed their organizations through periods of significant change, perhaps brought about by rapid changes in technology, competition, economic trends, and social changes and so on. They found that these leaders had managed change through three stages:

1. **Recognizing the need for change.** CEOs saw themselves as change agents with the responsibility for pointing out to the organization how it must change. They tended to encourage dissent, engage in objective assessment of the organization, and benchmark their organization against others.

2. **Creating a vision for change.** The vision was created not as an individual act of supremely creative inspiration, but rather by bringing together different viewpoints within the organization. This was seen to create a roadmap for the future, which employees were eager to support.

3. **Institutionalizing the change.** This involved the hard work of breaking down old methods and structures and finding people who were willing and able to develop new ones. New groupings were often required, and people were helped to find new roles for themselves that would support the new vision.

Transformational leadership appears to succeed because it empowers employees, causing them to set and achieve higher aims. In order to create the vision and implement the change, they tend to be open to dissent and feedback, be role models for their beliefs, and be seen by followers as articulate, competent and trustworthy. Followers appear not only to want to support the goals set forth through the transformational leadership process but, indeed, to emulate the leader.

4.5 Charisma and transformational Leadership:

Special gift that certain individual posses giving the ability to do extraordinary things. It is amongst the most important of transformational leadership.

4.5.1 Characteristics of a transformational leader:

Charisma can only be validated through the actions of the followers.

House identified the characteristics of charismatic leaders as including dominance, a strong desire to influence others, a strong sense of one's own moral values, and self-confidence. According to Meindl (1990), charismatic leaders tend to emerge in times of social and political crisis when there is a great deal of psychological insecurity and lack of social cohesion. It would seem that, when times are troubled, people look for a charismatic leader to come to their rescue and resolve disharmony. House agreed that charismatic leaders are more likely to arise in times of distress and that, in addition to certain personality characteristics, they also exhibit certain behaviors:

- Charismatic leaders set high expectations for their followers, with an accompanying confidence that the followers can meet those expectations.

- The goals tend to have moral or ideological overtones, providing a sense of a higher purpose.

- Charismatic leaders are strong role models for those beliefs.

- Charismatic leaders appear to followers to be very competent.

Finally, House points out that the result of charismatic leadership is that followers feel great warmth for the leader, congruence with and trust in the leader's beliefs and an unquestioning acceptance of the leader – and, of course, followers believe that their goals are worthy and achievable. According to House *et al.* (1991), charismatic leaders often:

- are perceived as having a divine or semi divine quality;

- have an unconditional acceptance of their authority and emotional commitment;

- have 'hypnotic' eyes and voice;

- possess good oratory skills.

4.5.2 Behavior attributes of charismatic leaders:

Conger and Kanungo developed a model focusing on several behavioral stages that:

Stage 1: The leader develops a vision of idealized change that moves beyond the status quo, e.g. J. F. Kennedy had a vision of putting a man on the moon by the end of the 1960s. Initially to most people this seemed an impossible task.

Stage 2: The leader communicates this belief and vision, and motivates followers to go beyond the status quo and visualize this happening.

Stage 3: The leader builds trust by exhibiting qualities such as expertise, success, risk taking and unconventional actions.

Stage 4: The leader demonstrates ways to achieve the vision by means of empowerment, behavior modeling for followers, etc.

Similarly, Conger and Kanungo (1998) describe five behavioral attributes of charismatic leaders:

- Vision and articulation;
- Sensitivity to the environment;
- Sensitivity to member needs;
- Personal risk taking;
- Performing unconventional behavior.

The research on successful leaders does not, however, universally support charisma as a necessary quality for leadership success. Collins points out that companies with charismatic leaders (for example Lee Iacocca at Chrysler) tended to decline after the leader left, because they tended to lead through strength of personality cult rather than through a strong leadership team.

4.5.3 Leadership Distance and Followers Perceptions:

Boas Shamir (1995) has suggested that notions of charisma may be different depending on how close one is to a leader.

Table 4.2   Followers views of close and distal charismatics

Distal charismatics	Common to both distal and close charismatics	Close charismatics
• Persistence	• Self-confidence	• Sociability
• Rhetorical skills	• Honesty	• Expertise
• Courage	• Authoritativeness	• Humour
• Ideological orientation	• Sacrifice	• Dynamism
		• Intelligence
		• Physical appearance
		• Setting high standards
		• Originality

4.6 Developing Transformational Leadership:

Bamberger and Meshoulam (2001) have argued that organizations can either make or buy transformational leaders. The more viable practice for most organizations is to train and develop transformational leaders internally. Bass (1990) proposed two methods for transformational leadership training:

1. **Individual coaching.** The MLQ is completed by a manager's line reports. The ratings are collected and presented to the leader in an individual counseling session and compared with self ratings. The leader is given personal feedback and target goals are set.

2. **Group workshops.** A group of leaders attend a workshop which incorporates the following activities:

   - Brainstorming the behaviors displayed by effective and/or ineffective leaders.

   - This is then linked to concepts of transformational leadership theory.

   - Participants watch videos depicting a variety of leadership styles in action.

   - Action plans are developed

4.6.1 Developing Transformational Leadership with Emotional Intelligence:

Individuals who are emotionally intelligent possess the ability to understand themselves and others, and are able to adapt their behaviors to a given context. There have been several recent studies (e.g. Duckett and Macfarlane, 2003) that have confirmed that emotional intelligence is associated with transformational leadership and increased performance. Additional research has shown (Slaski and Cartwright, 2003) that emotional intelligence can be developed through training programmes.

4.7 Concerns About Transformational Leadership:

Concerns range from its misapplication to its conceptual clarity.

4.7.1 Unethical Charismatic Leaders:

A key concern about situational leadership is that leaders whose success comes through a great deal of charisma may be more able to abuse the power they are granted by their followers. Because of this exceptional ability to influence others, and in spite of their emphasis on a sense of 'higher purpose', charismatic leaders may be successful in persuading followers toward ends that is not in the followers' interest.

4.7.2 Charisma May Not Be Sustainable:

The use of charisma is quite central to the transformational leadership process. Conger and Kanungo (1988) assert that charisma is not magical but can be learnt through training. But charisma may be difficult to sustain on a day-to-day basis. Charisma is more often associated with change agents than with those maintaining the status quo.

4.7.3 Does Transformational Leadership Focus Too Much on the Top?

Another criticism of transformational leadership is its focus on leadership at the top, perhaps to the exclusion of others. The leader is seen to be a visionary, and even though others may be involved, the leader is too often seen as the change agent, the one who has created and pursued the vision. Therefore the concern is that it is elitist, even antidemocratic.

4.7.4 Transformational Leadership's Lack of Conceptual Clarity:

A final weakness is in the conceptual clarity of the transformational leadership theory itself. The theory is extremely broad based, including envisioning, managing change, nurturing, being a social architect, being charismatic and so on. Its parameters are difficult to define, as it overlaps with so many other concepts of leadership. It also tends to contrast transformational leadership with transactional leadership on an either–or (or even good–bad) basis, rather than as a matter of degree.

Transformational Leadership in Context. One of the strengths of transformational leadership theory is the view that leadership is a process between two individuals – the leader and the follower – and the needs of both parties are to be met. The theory has intuitive appeal as well. People are attracted to leaders who can paint a vision for the future that will involve and benefit us all.

Learning Summary: Chapter 4

- Transformational leadership theory grew from concerns about the failure of traditional leadership practices in settings such as the war in Vietnam and the development of flatter organizational structures.

- Transactional leadership relies on the rewards that leaders can provide to followers through their position in the organization.

- Transformational leadership is in contrast to transactional leadership in that the focus is on the emotions of the follower, winning hearts and minds.

- Transformational leaders are described as charismatic and inspirational; they are intellectually stimulating and show consideration.

- Influential research of top executives who have been seen to be successful in the management of large-scale change has found that they tend to employ transformational leadership methods.

- Charisma is a key attribute of transformational leaders.

- Success has been noted in developing transformational leadership skills, both through individual coaching and through group learning experiences.

- Some of the concerns about transformational leadership theory are that charismatic leadership can be abused, that the theory may focus too much on the executives in organizations at the expense of other levels of leadership, and that it lacks conceptual clarity because it is so all encompassing.

5

Leadership: A Cultural Construction?

Learning Objectives

- Acknowledge the complexity of the constructs of culture;

- Consider the idea of culture of organizations;

- Understand linkages of leadership and national culture;

- Consider the linkage of leadership and organizational culture;

- Understand whether leaders can affect organizational culture;

- Consider leadership in different sectors: private; public and voluntary.

5.1 Introduction:

Can leaders and managers choose and then implement a corporate culture? Second, can such a culture survive or persist in a national or regional culture if it is not aligned with it? Third, can transnational or multinational organizations choose a culture from the very many in which their staff live, and if they can, how should they do it?

5.2 Culture:

Culture is that complex whole which includes knowledge, belief, art, morals, law, custom and any other capabilities and habits acquired by man as a member of society. The *Oxford English Dictionary* defines culture as a particular form, stage or type of intellectual development or civilization in a society, and also as a society or group characterized by its distinctive customs, achievements, products, outlooks etc. one culture does affect another. This happens by processes of diffusion across boundaries through trade, travel, alliances, proselytisation and so on. Also, cultures diffuse through conquest and colonization. Orgs can have a micro culture inside tier culture.

5.3 Culture of Modern Organizations:

Cultures (sometimes referred to as social structures) shape and condition how organizations are constructed and emerge. Our view is that organizations are manifestations of the sociocultural system in which they are embedded. This view is similar to the stance of Scott (1995), where he argues that organizations are the places where the social institutions of values, beliefs and modes of order can be observed and be seen to change. Hofstede selected four traits and argued that sets of traits could be found in different configurations. Hofstede's theory is justly famous for its cross-cultural focus, its simplicity and its boldness. The four traits he focused upon were:

• **power distance**: the degree to which organizations were hierarchic;

• **uncertainty avoidance**: the degree to which individuals preferred to avoid uncertainty;

• **collectivism**: the degree to which individuals subordinated individual preferences to the collective will;

• **masculinity**: the degree to which male characteristics were preferred over feminine characteristics.

5.4 Leadership and Culture:

Robert House has coordinated a major research project on cross-cultural leadership, GLOBE (Global Leadership and Organizational Behavior Effectiveness Research Project)

Power distance in society has an impact on different aspects of leadership. It seems that an autocratic style of leadership is positively related to high power distance. In countries with low power distance people prefer egalitarian leadership. In high power distance countries people prefer leaders who are less participative and more authoritarian and directive. And these leaders are perceived to be more effective in each context.

Uncertainty avoidance. In high uncertainty avoidance countries leadership is by planning. In low uncertainty avoidance countries flexibility and innovativeness are preferred.

Collectivism and individualism. Collectivism was found to be related to affective aspects of motivation to lead (Chan and Drasgow, 2001), and related to preference for transformational leadership (Jung and Avolio, 1999); individualists preferred a transactional leader. Dickson *et al.*, (2003) note that the terms 'individualism' and 'collectivism' have been regarded as too simple. They introduced two concepts on collectivism: vertical and horizontal. The vertical dimension was associated with power distance being high, and horizontal collectivism was associated with power distance being low.

Masculinity and femininity. Hofstede (1998) reconsidered these dimensions. The GLOBE project measured these aspects in a new way. First, they considered **gender egalitarianism**, which, when high, endorses charismatic and participative leadership. Second was **assertiveness**, which is associated with effective leadership in countries such as the USA but not so in Korea or in other Asian countries. The other new constructs introduced were **performance orientation** and **humane orientation.**

In case you think that individuals can be free of culture, you might remember that culture is stronger than life and stronger than death, for it influences every aspect of our lives in it's taken for grantedness. House *et al.* (1997) suggested that there might be three propositions:

1. Leaders' behavior is congruent with the culture in which they are embedded.

2. Leader behaviors that are slightly different from the culture might lead to innovation and change.

3. Leader behaviors are almost universal.

Leader behaviors that reflected integrity, charisma, inspirational and visionary attributes were found to be aspects of outstanding leadership. Those that reflected irritability, noncooperativeness, egocentricity, a loner, ruthlessness and autocracy were associated with ineffective leaders.

5.5 Some Caveats:

In the studies respondents were invited to respond in relation to ideal leaders and not the 'real' ones they encountered. In addition (to studies such as the GLOBE project) there have been a large number of comparative studies that compare culture and leadership in pairs of countries or among small groups of countries. These have produced three themes:

- First, many scholars view leadership with somewhat universalizing constructs.

- Second, there is a local valuation of these constructs.

- Third, human beings as leaders in different cultures behave in very similar ways.

Table 5.1   National and organisational culture

	National culture is homogeneous	National culture is heterogeneous
Organisational culture is homogeneous	The domestic organisation: leadership is an accidental fit.	Leadership may or may not fit the organisation depending on agenda for stability and change.
Organisational culture is heterogeneous	The geocentric organisation: leaders have to learn to be culturally sensitive to others.	Transnational organisations: leadership is a very complex problem of awareness and is likely to be transcultural. Choice of leader is crucial.

5.6 Back to Organizations

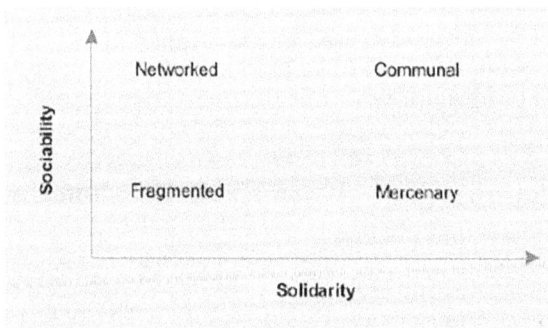

Sociability and solidarity

Goffee and Jones (1998) examined organizational culture along the two human dimensions of **sociability**: (the degree of friendliness between the workforce) and **solidarity** (the degree to which the workforce clearly understand and share goals). This produces a matrix of four types of organizational culture.

Etzioni argued that there were three ideal types of organization: **normative** (working upon and about values, close to the communal), **instrumental** (working at jobs in exchange for money, similar to mercenary), and **coercive** (working at what is commanded, like a prison). Most organizations are mixes of the normative and the instrumental, with some occasional lapse into coercion.

5.7 What Can Leaders Do About Culture?

Schein (1985) wrote of five mechanisms in use by senior managers to embed and transmit culture:

- chose issues to attend to, to be controlled and measured;

- reacted to critical incidents and crises;

- deliberately role modeled, taught;

- set criteria for allocation of rewards;

- set criteria for recruitment, promotion, retirement and excommunication.

Schein considered that the first of these was the best method for managers to communicate what mattered most. he also included the structures, information and control systems, goal and mission statements together with the stories, myths and legends that are told by the members and encapsulated into histories. Morgan (1986) in his images of organization provided a set of metaphors that could be taken to describe an organization. Among them were the **machine bureaucracy**, the **organism**, the **network** (or maze), the **psychic prison**, and the processes of **flux and transformation**. psychic prison represents an organizational culture where anxiety has become so high that the defenses of repression have been mobilized to deal with it, imprisoning the members in their unhappy condition.

5.8 Leadership In Private, Public And Voluntary Organizations

Private - subject to private interests and private objectives and goals, e.g. achieving the maximum value for the owners subject to all the environmental and market constraints. leader role here is essentially instrumental, a kind of task master. Leadership is resource dependent, on money, opportunities and capability. Leaders face the danger of confusing short-term, medium term and long-term goals and the behaviors that sustain them.

Public – Have multiple goals in conflict. Must be responsive to private interests and public concerns. Because they are public, they are open to more demands for transparency, accountability and control

Voluntary – Three types.

1. Values centered – i.e. religious. Leaders symbolize the basic values that they must not betray.

2. Service Orgs. – i.e. red cross Leaders are concerned with needs of actual and potential clients and the quality and range of given service delivery. Also face the complexity of leading a mix of professional staff, employed staff and volunteers.

3. Campaigning Orgs – Set out to change societies and laws. (political parties, issue groups) Leaders must be able to present the issues to the world and be articulate and probably charismatic.

You should note that national cultures and organizational cultures are not static, for though they are persisting they are also changing in small ways all the time.

Learning Summary: Chapter 5

- Culture is a very complex idea and has many definitions that include values, language, beliefs, customs etc.

- National culture and organizational culture are not necessarily the same.

- The idea of an organizational culture complex is a useful tool: the traits are ways of doing things, attitudes, behaviors and beliefs exhibited in an organization.

- In the field of leadership studies there are 'gurus' who act as symbolic leaders for managers.

- National culture (and organizational culture) were defined by Hofstede along four dimensions: power distance, uncertainty avoidance seeking, collectivism individualism and masculinity femininity. Hofstede found clusters of countries with similar scoring on the scales.

- The Globe studies found clusters of cultures: there were five European clusters together with a cluster of Confucian Asia, Latin America, Middle East, Southern Asia and Sub-Saharan Africa.

- Leader behavior was found to be congruent with culture in which it was embedded.

- However, there were found to be some universal aspects of (a) outstanding leadership; integrity; charisma; inspirational and visionary attributes, and of (b) ineffective leadership; irritability; egocentricity, ruthlessness; autocracy; being a loner.

- The fit of leader, organization and culture is very complex and has yet to be very well understood.

- Leaders cannot do much about national culture or regional culture. However, leaders can affect the cultural complex and thereby enhance performance.

- The key difference between voluntary, public and private organizations centers upon the degree to which leaders may define goals for participants. In voluntary organizations people join because of values: in public organizations values are plural, while private organizations can have narrower values and goals. The freedom of leaders to focus values differs in each kind of organization.

*Leadership is the art of mobilizing others to want
to struggle for shared aspirations.*

Kouzes and Posner

6

Gender and Leadership

Learning Objectives

- The recent presence and the prior marked absence of female voices in organizational leadership;
- The research debates and findings on how men and women leaders are necessarily different;
- How these research debates and findings relate to leadership theories;
- How women cope with male organizations;
- That organizational demographics might explain gender similarities;
- The pursuit of wisdom in leadership.

There are three arguments for changing towards including women in leadership:

1. Organizations are the poorer for not having all that female talent and capability. A subversion of this is that the trend to flatter organizations and more networking means that organizations should make use of women's skills of relationship to lead effectively.

2. Argument is a moral (or ethical) argument from concepts of justice and equality. This arguments asserts that women are equal to men in moral worth and hence should have the opportunities to work and lead in their ways, and men should adjust to them.

3. Argument is that there are no essential differences between men and women in traits and behaviors, but there are important differences within any group of human beings.

Lorenzen argues that a woman in a leader position cannot surrender her femaleness. Lorenzen follows a traditional image of woman as being skilled in relationships and human development, but adds the important ingredient of being able to exercise authority.

Stanford *et al.* (1995) asked women leaders to describe their leadership approach – they said they were employee-involved management style; participating in decision-making; working within teams, preferred sense of power was of reward and personal power bases (including expertise), and not position power, emphasized the importance of the high quality of interpersonal relationships with employees, had a long-range view of the organization and its work, and encouraged employees to share it, were also effective communicators in the workplace.

Is Women's Leadership Different from Men's Leadership?

Appelbaum and his colleagues (2003) asked three questions

1. Are women's leadership styles truly different from men's? (YES)

2. Are these styles less likely to be effective? (NO)

3. Is the determination of women's effectiveness as leaders fact based or a perception that has become a reality? (NOT FACT BASED its socialization).

Appelbaum considered four approaches:

1. biology and sex;

2. gender role;

3. causal factors;

4. attitudinal drivers.

Androgynous behaviors are a mix of male and female. It was observed that male or androgynous behaviors were more likely to be identified by people as preferred leaders than female leaders.

6.3.1 Organizational Environment

Women may have been socialized within their broader cultural context into believing that they are less fit to lead than men. Hence their attitude towards leadership is lower than that of men, a kind of lower class. This second-level status damages women's self-confidence, when self-confidence is a good predictor of leadership.

6.3.2 Organizational Patterns

Shifting patterns of organization from hierarchic to more flexible and embedded firms operating in negotiated networks has led to the suggestion that the stereotypical female capabilities (interpersonal skills, communication, empathy, collaboration, conflict handling and negotiation) might be of more use than the male (competitive, aggressive, strategic planning and winning) and lead to higher effectiveness.

6.4 How Do Women Cope With Male Organizations?

One strategy for women is to become like the men, but this leads to more discrimination and stress.

Eagley and Johnson found that women were more attuned to personal relations and democratic style, men to task achievement and autocracy. These differences were supported by Carless (1998), where it was observed that women were more likely to be viewed as transformational, participative, nurturing, praising, inclusive and considerate. Men were seen as directive, task oriented and controlling.

Power – if men are more autocratic and directive than women, it may be argued that femaleness is the likeliest true leader, whereas maleness is a wielder of power. In their study Stoebert *et al.* found that women scored higher than men on consideration but lower than men on reward and expert power.

Emotional intelligence - Mandell and Pherwani (2003), who found that emotional intelligence was a strong predictor of the use of transformational leadership style gave further quite surprising evidence of the relevance of traits to behavior. It could be concluded that men and women could choose to have emotional intelligence, but it is often asserted that women are more likely to possess high levels of emotional intelligence than men.

6.5 Demographics

Kakabadse and his colleagues concluded that men and women are just as effective. Women face hurdles in getting to the senior levels, but once in senior jobs their behavior was not different from that of men. But a further caveat to these studies might be offered, which is that both were conducted in the public services. Such organizations typically have overt antidiscrimination policies, but also may attract men with lower masculinity characteristics and a more androgynous gender orientation. If so, the evidenced differences between men and women would be unlikely to be present. The small proportion of women might also have skewed the statistics.

6.6 Do Women Make Better Leaders Than Men?

Pounder and Coleman (2003) answered this question as depending upon:

- **National culture.** Leadership style may reflect the national culture within which it is enacted.

- **Socialization (society).** An individual's particular style of leadership may originate in a variety of societal experiences, including stereotyping, that have shaped that individual's values and characteristics.

- **Socialization (workplace).** An individual's leadership style may shaped by the workplace experiences peculiar to that individual.

- **Nature of the organization.** It may be that differences in organizational type give rise to differences in leadership style.

- **Organizational demographics.** Factors such as tenure in the organization and in the job, experience of senior management responsibilities, and the composition of the managerial peer group may all contribute to the enactment of a particular style of leadership.

Emotional intelligence - it is importamt to understand again that judgment is more important than decision, and that good judgment comes from that strange human quality, wisdom.

6.7 Wisdom in Leadership

Wisdom is not merely that of the wise person who knows herself – not just the quality of knowing everything deep inside your soul about the human foulness in yourself. It *is* that, but it is also knowledge of the grace in yourself as well as the muddle and confusion; but, more, it is for leaders the quality of systemic wisdom that looks across the social systems and finds a route to understanding. challenge of systemic wisdom – to think about the whole system.

Learning Summary: Chapter 6

- The increase in the number of women in leadership positions has been a relatively recent phenomenon. However, the position and rate of change of position of women varies widely across the countries of the world.

- The voices of women differ from those of men but also differ between women from different countries and backgrounds.

- There is a difference to be observed between sex and gender roles; sex roles are biological and gender roles are socially and culturally determined.

- The masculine culture of organization creates a double bind for women; behave like men in order to succeed and if you do you surrender the female gender role.

- There is evidence that country culture shapes how leadership is understood; masculine cultures stressing such items as individualism, independence, and defined and separate sex roles. Feminine cultures had definitions including: involvement, community, and lower aggressive behaviors. Nevertheless, note that the culture descriptors are gender related.

- Men superiors have a different view of 'glass ceiling' than female subordinates. If male superiors are not aware of the differences in leader behavior of women then they will define leaders in masculine terms and hence exclude women.

- There is evidence that women's leadership styles are different from those of men. Women are likely to have higher emotional intelligence and a greater likelihood of using transformational leadership styles. However, this evidence is contested in a number of studies.

- There is evidence that societal and organizational demographics are strong determinants of both men or women leader behaviors and that men and women leader behaviors are very similar.

- It is argued that, because of culture, and hence expectations, men will be viewed in many masculine countries and organizations as better leaders than women will. However, it is not universally true.

- The rapidly emerging change in the complexity and instability of markets and organizations driven by ICT and globalization makes new and more difficult demands on leaders. It is argued that neither men nor women have a monopoly of wisdom, a leader quality needed in the new circumstances. Perhaps the observed androgynous leadership is better equipped to flourish in this new world.

7

Developing Ethical Behaviour in Leaders

Learning Objectives

- Define the term 'ethics' in relationship to a leadership context;

- Differentiate between ethical behavior and legal behavior;

- Describe an ethical dilemma;

- Identify a number of ethical dilemmas that typically confront today's organizations;

- Decide how ethics should impact on the profit motive in organizations;

- Understand the role of ethical statements, values statements, whistleblower policy and leadership in supporting ethical behavior;

- Define the difference between negative, congruent and positive ethical gaps in organizational philosophies;

- Describe the difference between ethical road maps based on principles, on outcomes and on moral virtues;

- Describe how ethical behaviors impact on effective leadership.

Ethics – study of moral philosophy – deal with abstract concepts such as: good, truth, justice, love, virtue, compassion, and ultimately what is right or wrong. Socrates felt that -One must be bound by morality – what is wrong or right, and must not be influenced by emotions or what might happen.

Morality is a social construct which existed before individuals or organizations came into existence. Ethically accepted practices vary across cultures.

Difference between ethical and legal behavior: Ethics and law are both moral conventions. Ethics are not legislated and are not punishable as lawbreakers. It can not be assumed that law abiding is also being ethical. Many civil protests have been because laws were seen as unethical.

Most ethical dilemmas are because of two competing ethical concerns and the judgment required to sacrifice one for the greater good of the other. Jackson stated that there are 2 difficulties in ethical business behavior. 1. Difficulties in identification or what is your duty and 2. Difficulties in compliance – doing your duty once you know what it is. So even when analysis is undergone to make an ethical decision, one must still face the challenge of putting that decision in practice.

Guidelines by nature are based on past experience and not particularly adaptable to new situations.

Code of ethics in business – some companies have created them but there is no evidence of that they actually practice it. Businesses are ethical only when the business leaders themselves act ethically.

Ethical behavior should be of concern only in as much as they affect profits. It can be argued that acting otherwise could be seen as neglecting the fiduciary responsibilities of management.

Table 7.1 Three propostions regarding ethical considerations in business

- Proposition 1: Ethical considerations are not of concern (as long as we are lawful) since they may actually interfere with profitability, and our first consideration needs to be to the shareholder.
- Proposition 2: Business is much more than a profit-making enterprise; it is a *means* for improving the lives of its stakeholders, therefore ethical considerations are paramount.
- Proposition 3: Ethical behaviour is a long-term business advantage: therefore, morality aside, good ethics is good business.

The Business Ethics Gap (Table7.2 Ethical stance in business)

The ethical position of the business	Example
Negative ethical gap: The organization positions itself so that it's ethical practices lag behind societal expectations and actively resists pressures, particularly as they effect profitability.	**The Ford Pinto:** Ford Motor Company chose to aggressively contest all lawsuits and legislation brought against it for culpability in the design and manufacture of gas tanks in its Pinto automobiles, which were prone to catch fire in rear-end collisions.
Ethical congruence: The organization identifies changing societal expectations and positions its products or service to meet those Expectations.	**The retail food industry:** As concerns grew about the food supply (preferring organic, avoiding genetically modified, being unhealthy in other ways) food producers developed product lines in response to those concerns. Such products often command a premium price.
Positive ethical gap: The organization positions itself so that its ethical practices exceed societal expectations, actively setting a standard and perhaps providing leadership in The development of ethical practices.	**Volvo and safe cars:** Volvo adopted safety as its ethos, in its products as well as all of its processes. It began making its cars safer long before safety standards were legislated by governing bodies. For example, seat belts were introduced in 1959 but were not required in weden until 1975.

A Road Map To Ethical Decisions:
Table 7.3 Three alternative roadmaps for ethical decisions

Type of unethical roadmap	Advantages	Disadvantages
Deontological/Contractarian: Ethical decisions are made against relatively unchanging principles that set out rights, roles and duties. Contractarian theory would dismiss any consequential damage of ethical choices as long as the choice was consistent with agreed principles. Unfortunately, such consequences may well be morally unacceptable. It is unrealistic to attempt to justify standing by principles, regardless of the outcomes.	Such principles can be well understood and interpreted, and what is 'right' can be clearly defined.	Outcomes are not considered: adherence to principles could lead to a lesser good.
Utilitarian/outcome morality: Ethical decisions are made based on outcomes, the path which will likely lead to the greatest good.	Flexibility in ethical Decision-making will lead to the best outcome.	The processes are notconsidered, so even unethical or unlawful means of achieving the best outcome can be employed.
Moral judgment: Ethical decisions are made based on internal moral virtues that support a life worth living. These two dimensions lead to the identification of character traits or virtues. The social dimension is based on the fact that we need to live in a community. The virtues of the Social dimension promote peace in the community. By contrast, the aspirational virtues promote inner peace. They are what help differentiate humans from other community dwelling creatures, for they give us the sense that we have space to accomplish something, to find a purpose for our lives, to develop a sense of personal fulfillment. The virtues associated with the aspirational dimension include prudence or sensibility, ambition, enthusiasm, modesty and self knowledge.	Ethical decisions rest on internal strength of character traits and morality, and balance emotion and judgment	Methods to assess and develop internal virtues are not well established and decisions must still be made within an xternal context.

Leadership and ethical behavior:

It is very clear that the actions of organizational leaders impact on the resultant behaviors of their employees. It is the leaders who have the ability to establish and communicate organizational values and then ensure compliance through the imposition of rewards and sanctions. When a leader is perceived to have a high level of integrity, the ethical intentions of his or her subordinates, whether they have strong moral beliefs or not, will be higher. **Advising and judging** are an important part of morality and implicit in the role of organizational leadership. By its very nature, ethical behavior is difficult to define, as most dilemmas are the result of two competing ethical considerations: both outcomes are preferable but not possible. Nevertheless, leaders' actions, or lack of action, will profoundly affect the ethical stance of their organizations. And the ethical stance chosen will certainly affect shareholders and stakeholders alike. There appears to be little doubt that good ethics is good business.

Learning Summary: Chapter 7

- Ethics is a branch of moral philosophy that can assist us, as organizational leaders, in making decisions about what is right and what is wrong.
- Behavior considered unethical, may not, however, necessarily be unlawful.
- Ethical behavior has two components: finding what is right, and then doing what is right.
- Mechanisms such as ethical codes of conduct and whistleblower policies do not appear to ensure ethical behavior; the actions of top executives, however, are effective.
- There is some support for the view that good ethics is a good long-term business strategy.
- Organizations may adopt an ethical stance that lags societal expectations, is congruent with expectations, or actually leads and perhaps influences expectations.
- A company with a strong ethical culture will probably find it to be an asset in coping with crises.

- Ethical decisions may be defined through three roadmaps: in congruence with established principles (deontological), in view of the outcome that is likely to be best (utilitarian) or through the character of the individual (moral judgment).
- Advising and judging are ethical requirements of the leadership function.
- Asking basic questions about whether an action harms people or the environment, affronts human dignity, provides personal gain or needs to be hidden will help us understand whether or not the action is ethical.

8

Leading Individuals and Teams

Learning Objectives

- Identify the different leadership concerns in leading an individual, in leading a team, and in providing leadership across a larger organization;

- Describe the components of the underpinning leadership behaviors involved in self leadership and transcendent leadership;

- Differentiate task oriented leadership behaviors from people oriented behaviors;

- Identify the developmental level of employees for specific tasks based on the situational leadership model;

- Choose the appropriate leadership style to match the follower's development level;

- Describe behaviors included in each of the four leadership styles: directing, coaching, supporting and delegating;

- State the advantages and disadvantages of overleading and underleading;

- List tuckman's four team development stages;

- Choose the appropriate leadership behaviors required to address each team development stage;

- Describe the relationship between team development stages and the employee developmental levels of situational leadership.

Leadership behaviors are strongly influenced by the individual leader's innate characteristics, experience and values. And leadership success is every bit as dependent upon the follower as upon the leader.

Table: 8.1 Three differing leadership requirements

Individual leadership	Team leadership	Organizational leadership
• One task • One person • One situation • Immediate timeframe • Leader focuses on • follower task • accomplishment • Psychological in nature • (Does not mean • micromanagement)	• Multiple tasks • Team or group • Several simultaneous • situations • Intermediate timeframe • Leader focuses on • success of the team • Is social, psychological • and involves group • dynamics • (purpose is helping teams succeed)	• Mission, purpose, vision, • strategy • Organization or community • Many simultaneous situations. • Long timeframe • Leader focuses on survival and • success of the organization • Political, historical, • sociological in nature

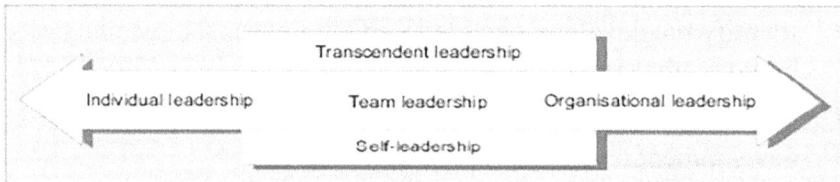

Figure 8.1 A continuum of leadership choices

Self leadership (self leadership is having the self-knowledge and self-discipline to select appropriate leadership behaviors even in the midst of pressures, crises and internal inclinations to do otherwise) **transcendent leadership**.(Transcendent leadership involves behaviors, skills and perspectives that are appropriate across all situations. Transcendent leadership applies whether a person is leading another individual on a single task, a team or a whole corporation on a complex strategic design or implementation. Integrity is the key transcendent leadership quality. - Tell the truth; - do what you say you're going to do. They are positioned in the figure to illustrate that they *underpin* the continuum of leadership and *are fundamental to all three areas of leadership behavior*.

Table 8.2 Underpinning leadership behaviours

Self-leadership	Transcendent leadership
• Any situation in which action is needed, the desired action is uncertain, self-confidence and motivation are low, and leadership by another person is unavailable	• Every interaction with every person, group, organisation or community
	• Every task, project, strategy, policy
	• Every timeframe from immediate to for ever
• Leader focuses on determining what to do and needs to muster the energy, spirit, strength, courage, drive and time to do it	• Leader focuses on internal congruence/integration
• Is psychological, spiritual, physiological in nature	• Espoused and operating values, behaviours, statements, etc.
	• Leader focuses on external congruence/integration
	• Shared visions, ideals, aspirations, values and joint action
	• Is psychological, sociological, group, spiritual, physiological in nature

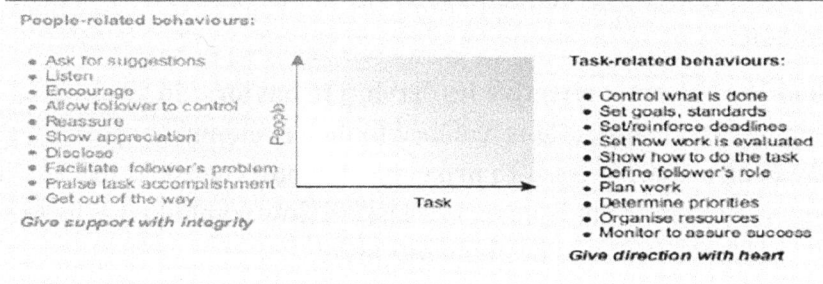

People-related behaviours:

- Ask for suggestions
- Listen
- Encourage
- Allow follower to control
- Reassure
- Show appreciation
- Disclose
- Facilitate follower's problem
- Praise task accomplishment
- Get out of the way

Give support with integrity

Task-related behaviours:

- Control what is done
- Set goals, standards
- Set/reinforce deadlines
- Set how work is evaluated
- Show how to do the task
- Define follower's role
- Plan work
- Determine priorities
- Organise resources
- Monitor to assure success

Give direction with heart

Figure 8.2 People-task leadership behaviours

Leading the individual: Importance of two independent factors in one-to-one and small group settings: consideration for the person, and task initiative. Consideration is sometimes called the **people factor** and task initiative is sometimes called the **work factor**. Each of these two factors is a group of related behaviors and concerns. Behaviors high on the people factor include support, encouragement, showing warmth, cooperation and caring. Behaviors high on the work factor include giving directions, following up to be sure the work is completed, planning the work for someone, and assigning work roles and responsibilities. However, a leader does not have to choose one factor or the other, for the two factors is totally independent. A Leaders Behavior and concerns may be high on one factor and low on the other, high on both factors, or low on both factors.

Situational Leadership: (SL) model better fits our experience in helping leaders to learn specific behaviors they can select to deal with employees. SL model recasts the two people–task factors as **support** and **direction**. **Support** is the people factor, defined as encouraging people, praising their good work, thanking them, helping them to solve their own problems, and so on. Its purpose is to build confidence, self-esteem and commitment. **Direction,** in line with the task orientation of the two factor model, includes telling and showing people how to do a task, being precise about outcomes, deadlines, procedures and standards, evaluating how followers do it, and monitoring their work. The purpose of the direction factor is to ensure compliance with appropriate methods and standards of working, and to build job related skills. In order to know what leadership actions to take, the leader must first diagnose the follower's level of development for the particular task under consideration.

Choosing the most effective leadership behaviors: In situation leadership the leadership style is matched to the development of the follower on a specific task. To make this diagnosis consider the following: How competent is he on *this* task? • How committed is he to *this* task? • How confident is he about *this* task?

D1 (Enthusiastic/unenthusiastic beginner)	S1 (Directing)
Follower usually approaches the new task as an enthusiastic beginner, unable to do the task but motivated to learn. he or she will need a considerable amount of control, but little support, beyond common courtesy	Would be clear about standards, targets and procedures while closely monitoring results and providing additional input **S1/Directing** • Leader has more control Support not required beyond common courtesy **Behaviors:** Control with heart, Give direction, Tell follower what to do, when to do it and how to do it, Monitor follower's work closely and constantly, Set targets and deadlines, Make decisions, Identify problems, control problem-solving and identify solutions, Define roles

D2 (Disillusioned learner)	S2 (Coaching
The employee may have begun the task with enthusiasm but then found thatsuccess has not yet been achieved. The follower may find that problems that were initially resolved reoccur or continued mistakes may have impacted on self-confidence Requires equal measures of support and control.	S2 may well be the most time-consuming style, as the leader will now also spend time reassuring and praising efforts as well as successes. **S2/Coaching** • Leader has more control, Support beyond common courtesy required **Behaviors:** Ask, encourage, control, Make decisions and set plans with input from follower, Explain decisions to follower, Solicit follower's ideas, Support and praise follower's initiative, Evaluate follower's work, Set goals and deadlines, Direct follower's work, Identify problems

D3 (Regular contributor)	S3 (Supporting)
Normally able to complete the tasks adequately but require support from time to time. The follower still needs reassurance and support but very little direction. Many employees may not move beyond developmental level 3; although they can consistently demonstrate the ability to do the task, they continue to require some reassurance or support from their leader.	The S3: Supportive style is required in this case where the purpose is to provide the follower with reassurance that work is up to standard and that the person is appreciated and valued. **S3/Supporting** • Follower has more control, Support beyond common courtesy required **Behaviors:** Ask, encourage, allow, Join follower in problem-solving when requested, Provide ideas and/or resources when requested, Listen to follower's ideas, Assure follower of his or her competence, Facilitate follower's problem-solving, Ask follower to define how task should be done, Help follower evaluate his or her own work

D4 (Peak Performer)	S4 (Delegating)
Individuals achieve peak performance – they develop high mastery coupled with high commitment and confidence in doing the task Individuals, often labeled star performers, are a most valuable part of any work team.	The only requirement as a leader is to delegate the task Nto the individual and then leave that individual to get on with the work. **S4/Delegating** • Follower has more control, Support not required beyond common courtesy **Behaviors:** Delegate with presence, Allow follower to set plans, solve problems, make decisions, Have follower evaluate his or her own work, Allow follower to take credit, Define problems with follower, Set goals together, Monitor follower's performance periodically or infrequently at most, • Be available to follower

When leadership styles do not match developmental levels:
Over leading (use of lower style than needed) and **under leading** (use of a higher style than needed). In some situations leader may find it advantageous to over lead or under lead.

	Over leading	Under leading
Advantages	May occur in times of crisis or urgency,	'Thrown in at the deep end', confronted a crisis or were involved in a startup operation with little or no guidance. All of these situations were times when the managers felt they were under led and had to quickly undergo a very steep learning curve.
Disadvantages	Entail giving more control or support than is required by the individual, the follower may well perceive such behavior as showing the leader's lack of trust in his or her competence, as being a 'control freak' limiting the individual's growth and de-velopment or even as being condescending.	The follower given too little control or support may well become discouraged, lose heart and Ultimately fail in task responsibilities.

LEADING A TEAM:

Team Stage	Member Behavior	Action steps to move ahead	Leaders actions
Forming	• Group members show courtesy towards each other and 'getting to know you' behaviors • Individuals share information and form initial stereotypes of each other • Individuals unclear on group goals pursue 'why we are here' discussions' • No conflict, but little productivity • Little trust or commitment to the group • Group norms and individual roles not established	• Set a mission, Set goals • Establish roles • Recognize need to move out of 'forming' stage • Identify the team, its tools and resources • Leader must be directive • Figure ways to build trust • Define a reward structure • Take risks , assert power • Bring group together periodically to work on common tasks • Decide once and for all to be on the team	• Provide structure • Hold regular meetings • Clarify tasks and roles • Encourage participation by all, domination by none • Facilitate learning about one another's areas of expertise and preferred working modes • Share all relevant information • Encourage members to ask questions of you and one another

LEADING A TEAM:

Team Stage	Member Behavior	Action steps to move ahead	Leaders actions
Storming	• Individuals push for influence • Cliques form, splinter, reform • Goals are set, changed, questioned, reset • Agendas are hidden • Some individuals unusually aggressive or passive • Conflict, even personal attacks • Problem-solving ineffective • Group accomplishments quite limited	• Team leader should actively support and reinforce team behavior, facilitate the group, for wins create positive environment • Leader must ask for and expect results • Recognize, publicize team wins • Agree on individuals' role and responsibilities • Buy into objectives and activities • Listen to each other • Set and take team time together • Everyone works actively to set a supportive environment • Have the vision 'We can succeed' • Request and accept feedback • Build trust by honoring commitments	• Use joint problem-solving, have members explain why idea is useful and how to improve it • Establish norm supporting expression of different viewpoints • Discuss group's decision-making process and share decision-making responsibility • Encourage members to state how they feel as well as what they think about an issue • Give members the resources needed to do their jobs to the extent possible (when not, explain)

LEADING A TEAM:

Team Stage	Member Behavior	Action steps to move ahead	Leaders actions
Norming	<ul><li>Roles, hierarchy and norms established</li><li>Start to view the group as a team; team identity established</li><li>Steady cliques have formed; members identify with the team</li><li>Creativity emerges</li><li>Team achievement is evident</li><li>Limited disagreement, 'groupthink' a danger, members don't confront to avoid 'rocking the boat'</li><li>New member entry is difficult</li></ul>	<ul><li>Keep up the team wins</li><li>Maintain traditions</li><li>Praise and flatter each other</li><li>Self-evaluate</li><li>Recognize and reinforce 'synergy' team behavior</li><li>Share leadership role in team, based on who does what the best</li><li>Share reward for successes</li><li>Communicate all the time</li><li>Share responsibility</li><li>Delegate freely within</li><li>Keep raising the bar/new, higher goals</li><li>Be selective of new team members; select and train to maintain the team spirit</li></ul>	<ul><li>Talk openly about your own issues and concerns</li><li>Have group members manage agenda fuss items, particularly those in which you have a high stake</li><li>Give and request both positive and constructive negative feedback in the group</li><li>Assign challenging problems for consensus decisions</li><li>Delegate as much as the members are capable of handling: team help them as necessary</li></ul>

LEADING A TEAM:

Team Stage	Member Behavior	Action steps to move ahead	Leaders actions
Performing	• Team members very motivated; morale and team pride are very high • High trust, intense loyalty, self-sacrifice for team good • No cliques • Individuals request feedback; no surprises • Confrontation seen as positive • All members accepted and valued • Superb goal attainment • New member entry may cause regression to a previous stage	• Maintain efforts that brought the team to this stage	• Jointly set challenging goals • Look for new opportunities to increase the group's scope • Question assumptions and traditional way of behaving • Develop mechanism for ongoing self-assessment by the group • Appreciate each member's contribution • Develop members to their fullest potential through task assignments and feedback

Learning Summary: Chapter 8

- Leading the individual is primarily psychological in nature, focusing on one task or situation at a time.

- Team leadership involves many tasks at the same time, and considers social, psychological and team dynamics.

- Organizational leadership is 'big picture' focused, uses influencing skills, and considers political, historical and sociological factors.

- In all leadership behaviors, there are two additional, underpinning leadership realms: leadership of self (managing personal energy and courage) and transcendent leadership (the key component being integrity).

- Leading an individual involves some level of both task focus and relationship focus.

- Situational leadership provides a model for selecting an effective leadership approach based on the development level of the individual. Individual development levels may be diagnosed by understanding the follower's competence, commitment and confidence for one particular task.

- As the development level is identified, the leader will then choose to use a corresponding leadership style: directing, coaching, supporting or delegating, depending on the follower's needs.

- Under leading or over leading an individual can have both positive and negative effects.

- Teams go through predictable development stages: forming, storming, norming, performing.

- The leader, as in situational leadership, can diagnose the team's development level and then choose leadership actions that will facilitate the team's growth to the next stage.

- There is considerable similarity between the team development stages and the individual development levels of situational leadership.

- Although the skills needed to lead individuals and teams are invaluable, additional skills will be needed in order to influence the wider organization.

9

Leadership Across the Organization

Learning Objectives

- Describe the situations in which organizational leadership skills are required;

- Identify the differences between organizational leadership and leadership of individuals or teams;

- List the five sources of social power and give examples of each;

- Describe a scenario in which a combination of social powers would be appropriate;

- Define the difference between power and influence;

- List the five leadership practices identified by kouzes and posner and several leadership activities that would support each practice;

- Identify areas in your leadership role where you can make better use of social power and influencing skills.

Although not in direct control of others' behavior, one must somehow find how to influence their behavior. To do so, it is helpful first to understand the ways in which power and influence may be projected within organizations. Having power over others in an organizational setting may be defined as the ability to have others modify their behavior in a desired manner, without, in turn, having to modify your own behavior.

Sources of Social Power - Type of Power	Example
Reward: providing something of value to an individual for responding in a desirable manner; Carrot part of the motivation. An incentive is a contract for performance: if you achieve this, the organization will give you that. It is in contrast to a reward, which may or may not be expected and is given after the fact.	• Pay, • Incentive schemes, • Bonuses • Verbal praise, • Gifts, • Symbolic rewards such as plaques, • Awards, etc.
Coercive: second part of the carrot or stick equation. the threat or application of punishment if the individual does not respond in a desired manner, often seen as the opposite of reward power;	• Threats of withdrawal of reward • Verbal (destructive criticism, bullying, etc.) • The disciplinary process • Ignoring, exclusion from the group • Assignment of unpleasant work • Discharge from employment
Legitimate: the 'official' authority conferred on someone as a part of their position of responsibility within the organization. Most effective type of power.	• Appointment to a management position • Active support from a senior person • Legally required such as internal auditor or safety officer • Membership of an external legal control entity
Referent: specific to the individual because they are well liked or admired (charisma and/or 'star' status are intrinsic to referent power);	• Someone achieving an heroic feat • Public entertainment 'star' • A 'star' within a profession or field of Endeavour • A highly charismatic individual
Expert: based on specialized knowledge needed by but otherwise unavailable to others	• Doctor, • Research scientist, • Building contractor • Engineering specialist, • Pilot, • Specialty consultant

Power vs. Influence:

Leadership can be exhibited, and quite effectively, by individuals who are lacking in virtually all five sources of power. This type of leader tends to serve as a catalyst and a facilitator, somehow making things happen but without needing to have a managerial job title, being charismatic or being an expert. Rather they tend to influence others by projecting a sense of **authority**, rather than by bringing a source of power to bear. Leaders such as these, who act with authority, are likely to use a coaching and consultative approach, providing equal measure of service and leadership: convincing, cajoling, praising, communicating, teaching, coaching, supporting, organizing and following up. They gain the support of others. This skill set seems more akin to influencing than to exerting power. In essence, such Leadership success will depend very heavily on influencing skills because, as we usually cannot command others, we must influence them to *want* to support our efforts.

Kouzes and Possner were able to formulate five **key practices** of exemplary leaders from the tremendous amount of data they generated:

1. **Model the way**. Set the example. Walk your talk. Be a role model. It reinforces our view that the key transcendent leadership quality is integrity. Integrity is built by keeping our word, being straight with people, doing things the right way, and so on. Leader's whole approach to business and people is values driven.

2. **Inspire a shared vision.** Successful leaders not only spend time creating a vision, but they do so in conjunction with their followers, developing a vision that appeal to the aspirations of the follower. Successful leaders also place a good deal of emotion into promoting the vision. It is precisely the process of being emotional that gives the vision depth and meaning. So the leader not only possesses a wholehearted belief in the vision, but he or she also preaches the vision at every opportunity.

3. **Challenge the process**. That successful leaders consistently challenged the status quo, and nurtured the same characteristic in others. They were experimenters and risk takers, taking time to question and explore alternatives, continually searching for ways to change and improve things.

4. **Enable others to act**. Empowerment is the key to this leadership practice. Delegation is a part of this process. Empowerment requires that followers need to feel they have the opportunity and power to act. Leaders can instill a sense of power and control

by allowing followers to make decisions. Indecisiveness is not tolerated while decisiveness is rewarded. The best performing teams are those in which the leadership function is shared.

5. **Encourage the heart**. Perhaps the most underutilized resource in today's organizations is the pride and enthusiasm of their employees. Conversely, goals and standards are clearly set at a high but achievable standard. And when those goals are met and exceeded, they are recognized and celebrated, personally and publicly. Followers of course want to achieve and feel that their talents are being well used, but they also want to know that their efforts are appreciated by their employing organization.

Leadership practice	Supporting behavior
Challenge the process	• Seeking opportunities that challenge and test skills and abilities • Keeping up to date on the most recent developments in the organization • Keeping up to date on the most recent developments • Challenging the methods, processes and procedures used at work • Looking for innovative ways to improve what is done • Asking 'what can be learned?' when things do not work out as expected • Experimenting with new approaches even if we might fail
Inspire a shared vision	• Discussing the kind of future to create together • Appealing to one another to 'buy in' to one another's dream of the future • Communicating positive and hopeful outlooks for the organization • Showing one another how their individual future interests can be served by enlisting in a common vision • Looking ahead and forecasting the future • Sharing excitement and enthusiasm about future possibilities

Leadership practice	Supporting behavior
Enable others to act	• Involving others in planning • Treating one another with respect and dignity • Giving people the discretion to make their own decisions and the training to make them correctly • Developing cooperative relationships with one another • Creating an atmosphere of mutual trust • Generating a sense of ownership among everyone over the work
Model the way;	• Being clear about philosophies of leadership, management and work • Breaking projects down into manageable chunks • Ensuring people adhere to the values and ideals to which have been agreed • Discussing beliefs about how to run the organization • Consistently practicing the values, ideals and philosophies espoused • Setting clear goals, plans and milestones for work
Encourage the heart	• Celebrating accomplishments when milestones are reached or goals achieved • Recognizing people for their contributions to our success • Praising one another for a job well done • Giving one another appreciation and support for their contributions • Finding ways to celebrate successes • Telling the rest of the organization about the good work we do

Learning Summary: Chapter 9

- Leaders often need to provide leadership across their organization, influencing individuals and teams from other areas, areas over which they have no formal authority.

- Organizational leadership is substantially different from individual and team leadership in that it may be required to consider organizational purpose, politics and history within the context of the wider community while involving any simultaneous situations within a longer timeframe.

- A model of social power includes five sources of such power: reward power, coercive power, legitimate power, referent power and expert power.

- Reward, legitimate and expert power may be viewed as positive and desirable methods to support leadership aims.

- Coercive power is not likely to be as effective, because of its unpredictable outcomes, while few individuals will find referent power to be a long-term source of support within an organization.

- Influencing skills are an additional source of leadership success in that they can be employed with little social power but also in conjunction with social power.

- Kouzes and Posner identified five leadership practices of successful leaders that any leader may successfully employ: model the way, inspire a shared vision, challenge the process, enable others to act, and encourage the heart.

- Organizational leadership and its associated influencing skills will be of increasing importance to leaders in the 21st century.

10

Leadership Development in a Fast-Changing World

Learning Objectives

- Identify the reasons why leadership development continues to be of great concern to most organizations;

- State how the focus of leadership development is moving away from developing individual leaders;

- List the six contextual changes that impact on the evolving approach to leadership development;

- Describe the implication of stratified systems theory for leadership development;

- Describe the implication of the theory of learning organizations for leadership development;

- Explain why leadership is moving from the individual to teams;

- Define a framework for developing the leadership function;

- List at least five components of the framework.

Many years ago – succession planning might as well have been called replacement planning as it was easy to look around the org and find replacement leaders. Requirements for leaders of tomorrow, their characteristics, attitudes and knowledge will be different from the requirements today. The search for corporate leadership has been largely unsuccessful.

The Need for a new approach - Leibman (1996) and his colleagues have pointed out that executives must modify their approach to the development of tomorrow's leaders – that the most important goal of succession planning must become the **development of strong leadership teams**. He described changes needed in succession planning methods, and named the new approach **succession management**.

Focusing on leadership function and leadership teams - focus in organizations must shift from a narrow goal of developing individual leaders to that of developing the leadership function and the team of leaders who will lead the organization through significant change. This shift must impact on everything from recruitment to succession planning, job placement, compensation and executive development. Viewed this way, succession management consists of two distinct but overlapping processes: identification and development. The purposes are to identify people who can jointly develop into better leaders as a leadership team and then to provide them with opportunities to develop their individual and shared leadership capabilities even further.

The changing context – why new approaches to leadership development are needed. – Six key forces are expanded below in detail:

1. **a change in the mode of conduct** required of leaders from transactional and transitional to transformational

2. **the need to change organizations,** but in uncertain ways;

3. **a change from heroic leadership** executed almost entirely by the individual to leadership carried out by leadership teams, teams that are cohesive, that have shared visions and which develop skills to complement each other

4. **a change from stable individual jobs** to strategic, constantly redefined tasks that are often performed by teams;

5. **a change from simple, logical, bureaucratic forms** of organizations to complex, global and organic forms, constantly coping with change;

6. **a change in followers** from industrial-era to knowledge-era mindsets

1. **From Transactional to transformational**: As proposed through transformational leadership theory, the focus of leadership actions becomes the follower rather than the leader.

Table 10.1   Contextual changes confronting organisational leadership

Traditional organisations	'New Age' organisations
Transactional leadership	Transformational leadership
Skill workers as costs	Knowledge workers as assets
Control driven behaviour	Commitment driven behaviour
Shareholder focus	Stakeholder focus
Managing stability	Leading constant change
Local simplicity (black and white)	International complexity (shades of grey)
Leadership by heroes	Leadership by teams
Hierarchical organisation design	Organic organisation design

2. **Need to change in uncertain ways** - the world is increasingly characterized by transformation rather than transactions. Therefore the organization is constantly changing – and in unpredictable ways. No job is the same, so the requirements for the individuals who fill the jobs are also markedly different. A traditional approach to succession planning falls short. Kur (1998), in his organization change work, wrote that it is useful to differentiate between two leadership worldviews:

   • those in which the leaders both know they must change the organization and have a vision of what it must be changed into; and

   • those in which the leaders know they must change the organization but have very little idea about what it must be changed into.

   Leadership development logically (or illogically!) demands that the organization somehow take on the almost impossible task of developing a range of unknown leadership skills that will serve the changing organization well under a variety of yet unknown scenarios.

3. **From Individual Hero to Team Player**: emulating the heroic figure is not an appropriate method to develop organizational leaders today. Such an approach may even be a distraction. In the best organizations, leadership teams are nurtured over years. Thus the development of the **leadership function** and the **leadership team** must be the focus of leadership development rather than the development of individual leaders. This perspective is related to what is sometimes called Super **Leadership** (Manz and

Simms, 1990). The focus of Super Leadership is twofold. First, systematically identify and develop the talent that each man and woman in the organization possesses. Then shape the expression of the talent within teams that synergistically pursue organizational aims.

4. **From stable individual jobs to Continually changing strategic tasks performed by teams** - in today's fast changing world few managers can describe their organization's environment as being stable, and would not anticipate stability at any time in the future. No future job will be the same as it is today, companies are looking at frameworks other than traditional in designing grading schemes and compensation for employees. Work is now being assigned to teams because of the increasing complexity of technology, markets, and so on. The ability to plan effectively for individuals to fill specific future jobs has been lost.

5. **From simpler to more complex more global enterprise** – some see a move to globalization as creating more organizational complexities – others argue that it will be simpler bur connected very carefully with simple work processes. It is not just globalization that makes development of future leaders difficult; it is also the increasing level of complexity in everything people do in every kind of work. Increasing numbers of organizations that have an 'organic' design, whereby teams, multidisciplined and fast changing, are assigned to a specific problem, product, or customer. The team may then, just as quickly, melt away as its purpose is accomplished and individuals are assigned to other teams to work on other tasks. In short, the ability to deal with complexity and ambiguity has become a central leadership requirement.

6. **A change in the nature of followers**: As information and knowledge moved to a central role in corporate life, the role of physical capital in determining competitive advantage declined. Information is a commodity that can be bought and sold. Consequently, it too has become insufficient to define competitive advantage. Collecting knowledge is the easy part. *'We're not constrained by information; we are constrained by sense making. We are not constrained by ideas but by what to do with them.'*

People capable of supporting the acquisition and management of information and of inculcating the development of wisdom and sense making around that information will be best able to lead organizations and it is equally evident that the followers, too, are different. As knowledge based workers, their expectations are of challenge, development, a sense of growth and contribution. The employer that offers such a place of employment will be able to recruit and maintain such highly skilled employees. If not, the workers can easily market their skills elsewhere (Q 12 Survey).

Emerging approach to leadership development – Industrial era organizations require employees who are specialized in the process. Todays; organizations find knowledge central to their success. Knowledge is difficult to account for and tough to organize. People employed due to their knowledge will require a different form of leadership than those employed for industrial-era behaviors. Increasing work will be done by teams – 2 theories:

1. **Stratified Systems theory (SST)** – Associated with Elliot Jaques. The idea is that leaders and others take action based not on what *is*, but based on their perception or *map* of what is. The implication of SST is that we must find ways to increase the cognitive capability of those who aspire to lead. People can increase their *use* of the cognitive capability they already have.

2. **Theory of learning behavior** - This theory proposes that organizations themselves must learn. Just as the human has the central nervous system to take in and synthesize information (the learning process), so must organizations develop a framework so that knowledge is gathered, retained and made available for later use. One principle underlying this framework is that becoming a learning organization requires an intellectual and emotional transformation of the organization's workforce. **Double loop** (method) learning is learning in which employees learn not only to behave differently, but also to think, value, and feel differently.

Frame work for developing leadership function of organizations: most leadership development programs will exhibit the following (5) characteristics in one way or another:

1. **a culture of leadership development, actively driven and supported from the top;-** process will probably start with the strategic planning process, where consideration of leadership development will be included as an enabling strategy and be a part of any SWOT analysis.

2. **leadership development aims that are woven into and evolve with organizational strategy;** although the link between strategy and environmental considerations such as customers, competition, technology and so on is usually strong, the link between strategy and leadership development is often quite weak. There may be several reasons for this weakness:

    a. It is conceptually difficult to link longer-term leadership development aims with the immediate challenges posed by the business environment. Therefore, leadership development is often focused on internal issues such as controlling costs, efficiency drives and team performance.

    b. The development of pools of talent can easily be postponed in favor of more immediate and pressing business priorities. In short, firefighting is a much more exciting and visible activity than fire prevention.

    c. Many of the forces described earlier in this module make it particularly difficult to bring a specific focus to the goals of leadership development when using the traditional classroom methods. In essence, the aim of leadership development is likely to be continually changing. (3M example)

Seibert *et al.* believe that the guiding principles for linking strategy and executive development are:

*   Begin by moving out and up to business strategy. The strategic directions of the business should drive the process of executive development.

*   Put job experiences before classroom experiences.

*   Be opportunistic, capitalizing on changes within the business environment.

Models of leadership development

The ladder. The most traditional of methods. Leader makes his or her way up the organizational ladder, one carefully defined step at a time. The only issue is how quickly the steps can be climbed.

The circus. Imagine a circus with its many highly specialized skills in and above the circus rings. This approach is one of increased specialization with little interaction with other specialties, but all performing at the same time.

The jungle. Leadership development here is based on the law of the jungle. The first goal is survival and the second is to best competitors to gain dominance. The most dominant gain promotion.

The N. matrix. Under this model, moving in any direction, up, down or sideways, develops leaders. The goal is that the diversity of experiences will better prepare leaders of today for tomorrow's challenges.

The academy. Based on the more formalized approach, found in academia, this process takes candidates through a series of rather formalized and lengthy learning processes, each resulting in tick marks on the CV. He or she with the most ticks is promoted.

3. Program aims based on competencies thought to be specific to the organization; Competency based leadership development systems have the potential to address the problem. most organizations begin by identifying far too many competencies, a result that makes the process practically unusable for most people. Brisco (1996) identified four approaches or 'foundations' that organizations use to identify competency.

Approaches to identify competencies	Benefits	Disadvantages
Data Based – based on superior performance in the company. Assumes what has worked previously will continue to work for future leaders	Has legitimacy as it is data based.	Competencies of the past may not be the one needed in the future
Value Based – Product of a strong culture or the vision of a specific individual (founder)	Quite motivational and tend to build and maintain the culture	Effective only if they are the ones that are most important to the org. Can sometimes be difficult to define
Strategy Based- identifies future requirements	Focus on learning new skills. Supports org change efforts	Difficult to define exactly what competencies will be required in the future. Selecting wrong may result in misdirection and wasted effort
Learning Based – requires leaders to learn quickly and adapt	Focus on basic and enduring personal skills.	May overlook established competencies also important to the business.

4. Support of leadership development through congruent HR and performance management systems; Internal selection, management development and reward system should be entwined with leadership development process to support and shape it. Most fundamental system required id Organizations performance management system. Meaningful development tends to be more in-depth. Other common systems are:

- **a job posting system**, advertising jobs that are available throughout the organization;

- **a succession planning system** whereby senior management reviews current and future leadership needs for the organization as well as the development needed by key individuals to fill those positions;

- **in-house leadership development resources**, which may vary from a relatively formal 'corporate university' to a less formal variety of workshops and training opportunities addressing a variety of topics in addition to leadership and management;

- **systematic executive involvement** whereby the executive team itself provides learning opportunities for junior leaders through activities such as mentoring, leading training programs, supporting secondments, facilitating the succession planning process and much more.

5. A broad interface with external resources. Traditional external source is university business school.

Evolving themes of leadership development – leadership will be more challenging and changing in the future. Orgs that meet the challenge will be most likely to succeed. Key to meeting the challenge is identification and development of leadership. As we strive to develop leadership effectiveness for organizations, the following themes emerge:

- The majority of an organization's leadership capability will need to be developed internally; it will not be feasible to acquire it from outside the organization.

- The process will need to begin with developing the leadership function in total, the system by which leaders and leadership teams are developed.

- Key skills will be the leadership of change, and in an uncertain world.

- Transformational leadership approaches that develop, enable and empower followers will be key.

- The ability to make the most of teams and networks will be of considerable importance.

- Leaders will also increasingly need to learn to deal with complexity.

Learning Summary: Chapter 10

- Programs designed to develop leaders have been available for at least 30 years and yet most organizations report that the need to develop leaders remains an exceptionally high priority.

- The reason why the need for leaders remains such a priority appears to be that the emphasis needs to be on developing leadership teams and the total leadership function, not just individual leaders.

- There are strong contextual forces that are shaping the ways in which leaders are being required to lead:

  - a move to a transformational style of leadership;

  - a need to lead change but in uncertain directions;

  - a move to team working and leadership teams;

  - a need to cope with continually changing jobs and tasks;

  - the increased complexity of global enterprises;

  - a change in the expectations of followers.

- Stratified systems theory supports the view that leaders must learn to deal with an increasingly complex business environment with many shades of grey.

- Organizational learning theory supports the view that leaders must engage the 'whole person' if they are to gain commitment rather than compliance from followers.

- Leadership teams are now required of organizations, rather than the heroic leader of times past.

- A framework to develop the leadership function must be enmeshed with the fabric of the organization, its leaders, its strategy and its HR and performance management systems.

11

Leadership Development Tools and Practices

Learning Objectives

- Make a judgment as to how much leadership ability can be influenced through a developmental process;

- Describe the behavioral choice model of leadership;

- Describe the main tenets of each of the six theories of learning presented in the module;

- State the role of hiring external people in the development of the leadership function;

- Describe the role of universities in providing developmental support for organizational leadership;

- State several methods of leadership development by job assignment;

- State several methods of leadership development by assessment and feedback;

- State several methods of leadership development by one-to-one support;

- State several methods of leadership development by structured learning programs;

- Develop a view on the effectiveness of the leadership development processes available in your organization.

How can leadership be learned? – Leadership success is a mixture of innate ability combined with experience. The would-be leader must have the intellectual ability to be able to understand the leadership task as well as some mixture of personal characteristics in order to interact effectively with followers. Given those basic characteristics, as with any skill, the emerging leader would also need to have the desire to lead, the opportunity to develop those skills and then the opportunity to be in a situation to apply those leadership behaviors.

Behavioral Choice Model: Kurt points out that any leader has a wide repertoire of behaviors from which to choose as he/she attempts to influence potential followers to align their activities with the purposes of the leader. When the leader chooses appropriate behaviors, followers choose to follow. Choosing effective behaviors is a process learned through experience and feedback. Behaviors that result in followers choosing to follow are retained and honed. Behaviors that are ineffective or even counterproductive are discarded. From this model, we can conclude that a motivated individual with basic abilities can learn to lead. Leader's success is also influenced by the context. i.e. success in one field does not mean success in another. **How do we learn?**

Learning Theory	Key points of leadership development
Behaviorism **(stimulus–response)**	• Concerned with observable inputs and outputs in learning • The theory focuses on the impact of external events (rewards) on the learning of behaviors • Rewarding behaviors reinforces those behaviors: thus learning occurs • Standards and goals should be clear to the learner • Feedback, clear and immediate, is key and is a type of reinforcement • For complex tasks, training should be structured in small, incremental • Steps, leading towards mastery of the task • Sporadic rewards are more reinforcing than consistent rewards • Ignoring behaviors will cause them to be extinguished in time • Punishment should be avoided as its impact on learning is unpredictable • A major step in learning theory, operant conditioning, was formulated by Skinner.

| **Cognitivism**

(mental processes) | • The theory examines the internal mental processes involved in learning (Herbert A Simon's theory)
• People have unique mental structures and will therefore learn in different ways
• Learning will occur through repletion and variety
• Concepts should be structured to present the same skill or concept in a variety of ways – reading, discussion, practice, observing and so on
• The development of language is a key support for increasing cognitive complexity and therefore leadership effectiveness
• Addressing subtleties and 'areas of grey' are important for complex skills such as leadership
• Cognitivist principles widely influence the learning processes today through techniques such as the use of discussion groups, presentations, written assignments, case study analyses, reflective writing and so on. |

Social Learning Theory
 	
(Monkey see Monkey do)
	• Sometimes referred to as the 'monkey see – monkey do' theory of learning, proposes that we learn through observing the behavior of others (Bandura, 1986).
	• The theory explores how learning can occur by observing others
	• Leadership skills may be learned by observing role models
	• If the role model is attractive, charismatic or admired, observed skills are more likely to be learned
	• Learning will be influenced by the treatment the role model receives for the behavior: the more positive, the greater the learning
	• Learning a skill does not necessarily mean an individual will use the skill
	• Learning must include 'cues' of when the learner is to use the behavior
	• There are several principles of social learning theory that apply to leadership development.
	
	  1. There is a difference between skill acquisition and behavior observer may well acquire the behavior without actually performing it
	
	  2. If the model possesses characteristics that the observer sees as attractive – power, intelligence, attractiveness, charisma, and popularity – the observer will be more likely to try to emulate the behavior than if the role model is unattractive to the observer.
	
	  3. The observer will be influenced by the treatment the role model receives for the behavior: if the model is rewarded, the observer is more likely to try to simulate the behavior; if the model is punished, the observer is more likely to avoid the particular behavior.
	• Social learning is seen to require four processes:
	
	  1. Attention is the first process.
	
	  2. Observer must not only recognize the behavior but also be able to recall it at the appropriate time in the future.
	
	  3. Observer must have the capability of performing the act, be it the intellectual, emotional or physical capability.
	
	  4. Observer requires motivation to perform the behavior.

Learning Theory	Key points of leadership development
Androgogy **(Adults learn differently from Children)**	• The theory focuses on how to make best use of the motivations of adult learners, setting the learner squarely in the centre of the process • Because adults learn differently, the structure and processes of learning methods should reflect these differences • Adults are most motivated to learn when there is immediate application of the skills, perhaps to solve a problem or assist with a challenge • Adults should help plan their learning • The teacher should be more of a facilitator, a peer assisting with the learning process • Learning processes should be built on the past experiences of the learner Knowles' principles of adult learning include the following: 1. Adults need to be involved in the planning and developing of their course of instruction. 2. Experience provides the basis for learning activities. Learning experience should be designed to build on the adult's prior experience. 3. Adults are most interested in learning subjects that have immediate relevance to their job or personal life. 4. Adult learning is problem centered rather than content oriented. Adults tend to attend learning experiences because they want to solve a problem or learn how to accomplish a task, rather than simply master a body of knowledge.

Learning Theory	Key points of leadership development
Learning Styles **(How individuals differ in learning styles**	• Advances the work of cognitivism by proposing four main learning styles 1. Activist, - important to have an experience. Prefer active learning 2. Pragmatist, - likes planning and testing new ideas. 3. Theorist, - likes to develop concepts and ideas 4. Reflector – likes to learn given the time to observe and then reflect. Avoid timed events. • The styles interact and a person can move through a cycle incorporating all four styles • In practice the individual is likely to rely on one or more styles more than others • Development should be structured to allow learning to occur via each style in order to reach all learners • Is a method for learners to assess and understand their own preferred learning style • Kolb developed a learning cycle in which he proposes that learners move through a circular learning process (see Figure 12.2). A learner could, in theory, start anywhere on the cycle and then move through the four phases in the process of learning the skill or concept.

Learning Theory	Key points of leadership development
Action Learning **(Learning by doing real projects at work**	• Revans creates a deceptively simple equation that states that learning occurs through a combination of programmed knowledge and the ability to ask insightful questions (L = P + Q). • Focuses on the optimum way to structure learning experiences • Learning occurs best when learners combine programmed learning with the opportunity to solve real-life problems in the workplace • Learning and problem-solving skills are typically enhanced through the use of learning 'sets' or small groups, which support each other in their learning and in addressing their projects • Team working, communication and feedback are skills that are learned through the sets in addition to technical problem-solving skills, all key components of effective leadership • Skills are learned by the individual, but the organization also benefits from the resolution of issues • The process of learning is generalized across the organization through the learning of many individuals • The process is well accepted in many organizations as well as in institutions of higher education •Several points from Revans' theory 1. The context in which action learning takes place is typically within the organization itself, 2. Two of the outcomes from action learning can be expected to be individual skill development in problem solving and the actual resolution of specific organizational problems 3. Generalization of the learning mode – organizational outcomes occur based on any number of individuals' learning 4. Many action learning approaches centre on small groups or 'sets' that support and critique each member's action learning projects.

Organizational Practices: Organizations can either bring people in from outside the organization or develop those employees internally. Offering promotion and development to existing employees is regarded as good management practice in order to build morale and loyalty.

Table 11.2 Organizational leadership development practices: advantages and disadvantages

Organizational ledership development methods	Examples	Advantages/ Disadvantages
Enrollment of leaders in university-based programs	• BA and MBA degrees • Executive development courses • Short courses	• Expert faculty • Currency of ideas • Well-designed curriculum • Cost may be more • Content may not be organization specific
Development through job assignment	• Rotation along career path • Secondments – assigning individuals to another part of the organization for a period of time and then bringing them back. • Job swapping – less costly • Job sharing – typically used to meet the needs to young parents • "back to basics" assignment – managers spent time on the floor – thought to keep them close to the customers, subordinates and the heart of the business.	• Provides unparalleled breadth of generalist knowledge • Host area gains as well as the individual • Organization may not be large enough to allow practice • Cost of relocation may be high and impact on the individuals family

Organizational ledership development methods	Examples	Advantages/ Disadvantages
Development through assessment and feedback	• Assessment centers – see Table 11.3 for components of assessment center. • 360 feedback • Psychometrics – self discovery and analysis • Performance reviews	- Provides clear feedback on traits and behaviors - Feedback is relatively objective - Participants tend to accept feedback - Costs may be high for assessment centers - Participants may become 'immune' if repeated over time
Development through one-to-one support	• Mentoring and shadowing • Coaching – one on one	- Protégé´s have one-to-one interaction with the executive - Opportunity to model leadership behavior - Mentors should be trained to optimize the experience - Time consuming for the executive - Depends on the 'chemistry' between the mentor and the protégé.
Structured learning programs	• In house training • E-learning • Corporate universities • Community service • Specialized programs • Health promotion – leader in good health are more productive • Employee Assistance programs • Learning centers	• Target specific development needs • Flexibility for learner to pick and choose • Relatively cost-effective • Requires resources to coordinate and keep up to date • Involvement may be scattered, lack cohesiveness

Table 11.3   **Typical components of an assessment centre**

Exercise	Description	Typical skills assessed
Impromptu speaking	Individuals are asked to speak for a short period of time on a randomly selected topic	Poise, the ability to think under pressure and public speaking skill
In-basket exercise	A number of work-related notes, emails, phone calls, letters are to be assessed, prioritised and acted upon within a rather short period of time	Business understanding and judgement, the ability to prioritise, delegation
Leaderless group discussion	The group is assigned to a problem or topic to discuss it and perhaps reach a conclusion	Group participation, leading, listening, assertiveness, team working
Team problem-solving	The group is assigned a task to complete (often a physical task such as constructing a display stand) within a given timeframe and 'budget'	Teamworking, leading, influencing, planning, listening skills, prioritising
Individual presentation	Each individual is asked to prepare a presentation on an assigned, usually work-related, topic	Planning, developing and delivering a more formal presentation, responding to questions
Report-writing	A set of business-related data is provided and the individual is asked to analyse the data and write a summary report, perhaps with recommendations	Data analysis, understanding of business issues, decision-making, written skills

Table 11.4   A 'three-track' leadership development design

Business track to learn about this organization	• Pre-residential workbook completion assignment • Week-long business knowledge residential course • Group case study • Formal inputs and interactions with expert speakers • Executive question and answer panel • Syndicate presentation to senior panel • Action learning project selection • Action learning project team formation • Action learning team member feedback • Project support workshops (financial analysis, presentation skills, project management)
Leadership track to develop skills in leading individuals, teams and the organization	• 360_ feedback and psychometrics • Week-long leadership institute • Learning team design (7–8 people) • Experiential learning exercises • Facilitator- and media-based presentations/inputs • Assigned readings • Self-analysis • 'Buddy' assignment for coaching and feedback • Facilitator feedback and coaching • Team project and presentations • Intensive team feedback • Selection of an 'at work' leadership project
Personal track to understand individual traits and behaviors for enhanced self- leadership	• 360_ assessment • Personal reflection and development planning • Psychometrics • Team member feedback • Coaching from facilitators • At-work application and reflection • Coaching relationship with their manager • Workshop experiences and exercises • Physical health assessment and improvement plan • Longer-term professional development plan

Learning Summary: Chapter 11

- Given the basic characteristics and a desire to lead, leadership skills and abilities can be enhanced through the learning process, by learning to choose to employ effective behaviors while avoiding ineffective behaviors.

- The learning theory of behaviorism shows that when an action is rewarded, it will tend to be repeated.

- The learning theory of cognitivism maintains that learning is a highly individualized internal process, and experiences are best structured to cater to individual differences.

- Social learning theory holds that learning occurs by observing others. Also, when the observed person is both attractive and receives positive feedback for his or her behavior, learning is more profound for the observer.

- Androgogy proposes that adults learn substantially differently from children, primarily because their learning needs tend to be immediate and task oriented: therefore learning activities should acknowledge this in their design.

- Learning styles theory illustrates a cycle of learning in which a learner might prefer alternate styles such as testing, experiencing, reflecting or conceptualizing.

- Action learning focuses on the process of learning, and holds that individuals learn best by confronting a real problem while, at the same time, being involved in a structured learning program to support the problem resolution.

- Methods by which organizations develop leadership ability include recruitment, offering in-house training programs, using university based programs, rotating job assignments, assessment and feedback processes, one-to-one support, and more comprehensive, long running programs that employ a combination of these methods.

- Leadership development in the future will rely less on classroom type development programs, instead moving to processes that rely more on thoughtfully selected development work assignments.

12

Strategic Leadership

Learning Objectives

- That three different strategy eras have shaped ideas of strategic leadership;
- The roles of the strategic leader – configuring, facilitating, delivering and evaluating (learning) and changing;
- The idea of strategic alignment and how to work with it;
- That the origins of strategic leaders are embedded in the three strategic eras.

A key aspect of organizational management is not only the choice of strategy but also the choice of the processes of strategy formulation and implementation. In the modern corporation strategy might take a variety of forms depending upon problems, history, technology and personality. Some authors differentiate strategic and managerial leadership:

12.1 Rowe (2001) claims that strategic leadership enhances the wealth creation process in entrepreneurial and established organizations and leads to above average results. In contrast, managerial leadership will achieve average returns at best and is likely to achieve below average returns and destroy wealth. But Rowe was careful to offer three interesting definitions:

Strategic leadership is the ability to influence others voluntarily to make day-to-day decisions that enhance the long-term viability of the organization, while maintaining results.

Managerial leadership involves stability and order.

Visionary leadership is an interesting third idea he added, which is future oriented and concerned with risk taking, and noted that such people are not dependent upon their organizations for who they are.

12.2 Strategy Schools

Coad (2005) has argued that it is useful to see that there have been three stages of strategic thinking:

The era of grand design and systematic planning; was about the content of a strategy, Environment ->Strategy-> Conduct-> Performance Design approach is clearly based upon an attempt to be rational and systematic in an uncertain, turbulent and risky environment. Its supporters do not claim that it was perfect, but that it was better than any process that did not include these steps. The critics claimed that this design process was an unhelpful bureaucraticisation of strategic management, which needed creative and innovative thinking. A sharper criticism was that the design school seems to be a good idea but:

- It overestimates the capacity of managers to handle all of the complexity and uncertainty at the same time;

- The real differences in views about goals and objectives as well as means would be stifled rather than examined;

- It reflected a narrow unitary conception of a complex organization;

- Because the timescales of analysis, feasibility and choice were very long, not only would opportunities in dispersed parts of the organization be missed but also the design would be reconsidered even before it had been actioned.

The era of strategic positioning; First era was about the content of the strategy - era not only built upon the first but also set out to establish that there were generic (or universally applicable) strategic positions: cost leadership; differentiation; focus. These five forces were threats from:

- New entrants; • substitute products; • customer bargaining power; • suppliers bargaining power;

- The intensity of interfirm competition.

By analyzing the value chain, and especially its linkages, it may be possible to see the basis of competitive cost advantage. However, Porter argued that there were only two sources of competitive advantage, from either having overall cost leadership in the industry or differentiation.

Miles and Snow (1978) offered four possible strategic positions:

- **Prospectors**, who were entrepreneurially exploring new domains;

- **Analyzers**, who were a bit like the design school prescription?

- **Defenders**, who were interested only in responding to strategic problems by protecting themselves; and

- **Reactors**, who were only responsive to others.

The era of complexity. Research suggested that any strategy was not so much designed but emerged from complex organizational processes and history. So strategies, even as attempts to be all encompassing, were built upon what had gone before. They were considered quite regularly), **remedial** (they were often triggered by problems to be solved) and **fragmented** (only parts of the organization could be considered). Both the design era and the positioning era, according to Coad (2005), emphasize predictability, order and control in a world of complexity and uncertainty. But the doubts remained about whether these approaches acknowledged enough of the uncertainty or risk, or paid proper attention to the aspects of organizational life that economics does not capture.

12.3 The Strategic Leader

There is a temptation to define strategic leaders in terms of their desirable traits (e.g. integrity, humility, intellectual capacity, action orientation, visionary capability, and strategic capability), their behavior and style, their charismatic and transformative behaviors...

Any role has the following three dimensions:

- That ascribed in job definitions;

- That of the interpretations of the role holder;

- The interpretations and expectations of the organizational members and stakeholders.

The elements of configuring, facilitating, delivering, evaluating and changing lie at the core of the strategic leader's role. Although we separate them out in a (hopefully) neat schema, do understand that they all go on all of the time in a complex organizational dance.

Configuring Strategy – more a process of configuration than a choice of decision-making. The role here is more of enabling the organization to consider its environment and its shifting characteristics. The role here is not to make decisions, as though organizational life was a business school case study, but to help the organization to form an appreciation (Vickers, 1965) of its setting and its possibilities.

Facilitating Strategy - key role of strategic leadership is to ensure that the organization has and can build capability through building resources, resource networks and their capability, physical assets, intangible assets and human assets.

Delivering Strategy - the third key role is of leading implementation to ensure that organizational programs and investment are aligned with the commitment of resources to programs.

Evaluating Strategy – Leaders need to consider four levels of evaluation:

1. **Compare** what was intended with what happened, and enquire into causes and meanings, in order to learn, but not to scapegoat or to punish.

2. **Consider the ideas** that informed the course of action, consider whether these were well enough understood, and seek gaps in understanding in order to consider how to fill them.

3. **Consider the debates** and analysis that took place and are taking place in the configuration process. What was included and excluded? What might be reconsidered? What new ideas might help here to reconsider the processes of configuration?

4. **Engage in dialogue** as much as possible with the varied stakeholders as to their perceptions and evaluations in order to gather the widest understanding

Changing Strategy – change is a normal expectation and not an admission of failure or incompetence. Change may be thrust upon the organization. Hence there may be a need to engage in crisis intervention.

This requires subtle skills, for others will be aware of the trouble and failure.

Power and Values - use of personal power is almost always immediately appealing to the leader but becomes destructive. Values lie so deeply at the heart of normative organizations that it is important to be careful with the ideas of leadership, for leaders here are the servants of the values not the masters.

It is an approach that sees leaders as acting out or through institutional norms, beliefs and orders and by their actions changing them in subtle and often invisible ways. It is an approach that does not decentre or devalue the person but does engage with persons as embedded actors rather than as naïve individualists.

12.4 Strategic Alignment –

Ensure all staff understand the strategy and their role in it, with subgoals	Internal marketing; clarity of regular communication and reporting of progress and changes	Survey of understanding Performance reports
Reinforce the sense of purpose and urgency	Regular briefings Maintain time pressures	Surveys of understanding Performance monitoring
Ensure corporate structures fit to strategy Teamworking	Redesign structure for clarity of implementation and collaboration	Review of problems of functioning
Fit control structure to strategy	Design control structure (planning, innovation, investment, budgeting) to enable strategy	Review of problems
Connect organisational culture to strategy Encourage an openness to learning	Develop organisational culture by example, by education and by local briefing Be open to questions and changed circumstances	Review of organisational problems, especially those that are about how the organisation connects to the outside world of suppliers and customers Track surprises Staff survey of climate
Fit rewards to desired performance subgoals	Modify incentives schemes	Payments of incentives in relation to performance; make this public
Encourage personal goals to be aligned with strategic future	Use staff appraisal to build staff development skills and competences in future capability	Regular HR reviews of staff capability

Alignment refers to the need to align the organization to the strategy. Clearly alignment is a major task of the strategic leaders. Common practice for companies is to develop mission statements.

1. Make sure the mission statement is the result of informed debate and fits in with managers knowledge of what is and what might be.

2. Ensure all employees have a copy explained to them.

3. Make sure they understand it.

4. Encourage buy in and commitment to the mission statement.

5. Ensure that actions to implement the changes are done.

Softball and Hardball – Stalk and Lachenauer (2004) argued that leaders have played too much softball and should learn to play hardball. They argue that softball is for losers

Work like this	Because...	Use these strategies
Focus relentlessly on competitive advantage	it can wither away.	Understand what this is and do it
Strive for extreme competitive advantage	you get out of competitors' reach	Continuous improvement
Avoid attacking directly	it's less costly and more likely to succeed.	Devastate rivals' profit sanctuaries Deceive the competition Plagiarise with pride Unleash massive and overwhelming force Raise competitors' costs
Exploit people's will to win	victory goes to those who want it most.	Reward the winners
Know the caution zone	you can play the edges.	Stay legal but don't accept conventions

Resistance – All proposed strategies meet resistance. Resistance can show up as over-dependence, conflict and diversion. Corporate leaders can use position power to override objections and objectors but persuasion and engagement may be a better long-term process.

The Long game – Strategic leaders must play a long game.

Summary – strategic leadership is understandable in relation to the three eras. Initially conceived as an analyst and planner, the strategic leader was expected to be able to use economic models to select the best competitive position and implement the choice. The third era of complexity requires the strategic leader to link strategy with a wider relationship to societies and governments. This requires the connection of strategic capability with a capability for policy formulation, working across the boundaries of the company and for engagement in the politics of public affairs. Competitiveness lies at the heart of all of the strategic leader's tasks. The leader has to ensure that the vision and goals are set, and that the systems for implementation are in place. The five roles in the strategic leadership cycle of configuring strategy, facilitating strategy, delivering strategy, evaluating strategy and changing strategy ensure that competitiveness can be built and maintained. One key aspect of strategic leadership is strategic alignment of the resources of the company in pursuit of the strategy.

The three strategic eras have different implications for strategic leaders:

- The design school approach would ask how to build strategic leaders.

- The positioning school would ask how to choose and change them in relation to problems.

- The complexity school relies on the capacity of talented individuals.

But all three require individuals to prepare themselves, in a critically reflexive manner, using all roles and events as opportunities for learning and development. However, leaders and managers acquire success at different stages of their lives, and there is some evidence that those who are best fitted to be generals of the competitive enterprise may not be the best equipped for the most senior positions where strategy has to be linked with policy. Also, experience is very context specific. It is difficult to learn enough about commercial organizations to be able to exercise leadership of them and in them. So perhaps strategic leaders' capability is sector specific. An implication is that organizations should resist importing leaders from quite different sectors. This conclusion agrees with the ancient Greeks' view that soldiers rarely manage the shift to political leadership.

Learning Summary: Chapter 12

- Strategic leadership is a central aspect of organizations, concerned with change, direction and effective implementation.

- Policy is about the affairs of the state and of the whole organization in its complex and uncertain context; strategy is about the choice of action. These words derive from ancient notions of political and military leadership.

- The three schools of strategy, grand design and systemic planning, strategic positioning and the era of complexity have shaped how the tasks of strategic leadership have been viewed. The earlier schools have not been superseded but coexist with the later.

- The grand design school tended towards heroic leaders. The positioning school tended towards analytic teachers. The era of complexity tends towards wise policy leaders. However, all three capabilities might be necessary in the future.

- Strategic (and policy) leaders must lead their organizations through the five stages of strategy: configuring; facilitating; delivering; evaluating; and changing strategy.

- A key aspect of the configuring and facilitating stage is strategic alignment of staff, culture, structures, control processes, operational goals, external and internal resources.

- In a competitive world, a strategic leader may gain strategic advantage by 'playing hardball' within the law to directly disadvantage competitors.

13

Leadership and Risk

Learning Objectives

- The ubiquity of risk and uncertainty;

- How risk is handled privately, publicly, individually and collectively;

- How risk stances shape the leadership of corporate risk management;

- Organizational risk management purposes and consequences;

- Socially and culturally shaped perceptions of risk;

- Organizational leadership in a risk society.

Introduction:

Developments on the structure and procedures of risk management approaches are useful and helpful. They are usually based upon, first, the creation of a risk register (much as actuaries and insurance firms do); second, a problem-solving first-order control loop (recognize, assess, consider choices, decide, monitor and review); and, third, a belief that organizations have enough information to make a choice of a risk profile. In addition, guidance can be provided for staff on how they consider risk in their decisions.

Uncertainty and Risk= we could formally distinguish uncertainty (about which we cannot assess probabilities) from risk (about which we can assess probabilities). This rise of modernist rationality, with its perception that adequate models of events could be constructed and probabilities could be calculated*, fitted the world as a closed rational system. Here lies the world of the risk management industry.* Calculations of risk were derived from centuries long development of the mathematics of probability, mostly in relation to closed systems, such as dice and playing cards. The later application of probability to real problems showed the limits of the models and more clearly the limits of any data that might be available as a basis for establishing probability distributions of real world events. Most of the time leaders are facing decisions about events that have unknown probability distributions, but to develop a calculus a model must be selected from which inferences may be drawn. The standard normal distribution is one such. Unfortunately, as the 'tails' of the distribution have the most inexact fit, the model is not good to use in the very areas of small probabilities of significant losses (or gains).

How Risk is Handled:

We suggest that risk is handled (and of course sometimes ignored) individually and collectively, publicly, organizationally and privately to produce six broad arenas, as in Table 13.1.

Table 13.1   Private and public individual, organisational and collective approaches to handling risk

	Individually	Collectively
Privately	Personal stance for risk-taking Gambling Entrepreneurship	Via families and communities Via insurance Via capital markets
Organisationally	As a leader taking the risk of new roles; of new business opportunities	Leading the organisation's policies on risk management; leading by taking 'risky' decisions for business advantage
Publicly	As a political actor as a part of strategic and policy leadership	Involvement in economic policy debates; regulation debates, trade negotiations

Individuals are the accidental holders of risk of poverty, illness, accident and death. Many things, including the cultural context within which an individuals born and educated, may condition the risk stance (see later in this chapter) of that person. But people come in many varieties, and in any country there will be a widely differing propensity to take risks. The individual risk taker in the West is called the **entrepreneur.**

Privately and Collectively: Here families and communities handle risk. These patterns can work within a country or across many countries and serve as a risk management process. Other ways of handling risk here are through many kinds of insurance. Also, financial markets can and do price risk and offer contracts at varying levels of risk. So losses can be protected,

Organizationally and Individually: Here we might be reliant upon membership of a professional body to establish codes of conduct and to arrange indemnity insurance. Leaders are very exposed to the quality of their judgments about how they frame policy and risk approaches. Being wrong usually means that the leader has to resign, even if no other person could have been correct (or lucky).

Organizationally and collectively: The leadership of risk management requires judgment of how much investigation we undertake and just how much uncertainty the organization can work with. It also requires leadership to ensure that there is no risk from failing to comply with laws and regulations.

Publicly and individually: Here we have the case of the political actor in advocating changes in policy of government in respect of economic structures, social arrangements and other laws. You might work as a leader of a pressure group, or in social activism for causes such as education, poverty or the environment. Or you might be seeking government support for measures to protect your firm from overseas competition.

Publicly and collectively: Collective public institutions are created to accept the task of provision to meet distress (e.g. health care, welfare and national assistance) and to ensure minimum incomes. Collective public regulations are enacted to provide protection. Governments also provide officers to enforce regulations, and courts where both private and public offences may be tried. A current issue is environmental degradation, where many governments have adopted policies of seeking to ensure that the costs of pollution are met, via fines and via the 'polluter pays' principle. Beck's (1992) argument is that none of these arrangements can cope with the changes imposed in the new risk society where the very risks to be faced are unknown and are the product of modernism; in his view the risk holders of last resort are individuals scattered about the globe, as indeed the risks are scattered about.

So far, risk has been presented as an aspect of events, but perhaps the social and cultural contexts might be more significant. So we now turn to a brief discussion of how risk is perceived.

Risk Management in Corporations

A review of Stances towards Risk:

Mary Douglas, an anthropologist, and Aaron Wildavsky, a political scientist, combined to consider a broad social insight into risk (1983). They derived a categorization of stances typically taken towards risk. These categorizations were derived from beliefs about the nature of the social world and beliefs about equality, as Figure 13.1 shows.

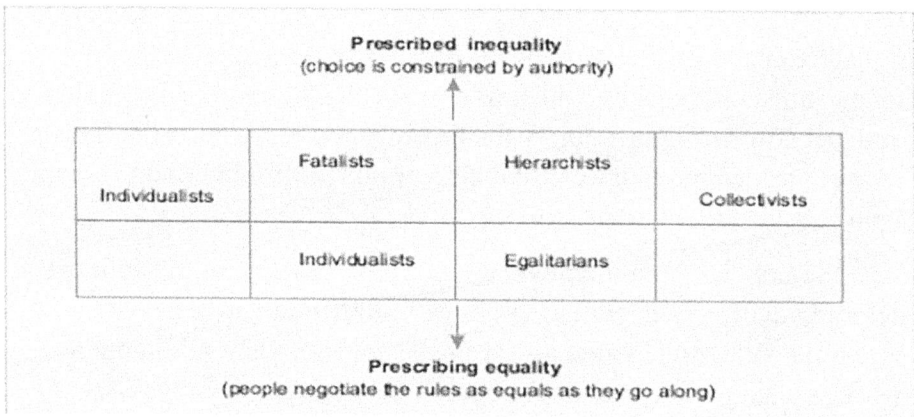

Figure 13.1 Risk stances

Adams (1995: 36), following Douglas and Wildavsky (1983), suggested that we might think of the four characteristic positions in the diagram as stances taken towards risk. These are as follows:

- **Individualists** are enterprising self made people, relatively free from control by others, who strive to exert control over their environment and the people in it. A good example is the risk taking entrepreneurial leader of popular capitalism, Richard Branson, founder of the Virgin companies.

- **Hierarchists** inhabit a world with strong group boundaries and binding prescriptions. Social relationships in this world are hierarchical. Leadership is about style or about working with contracts and transactions. Leaders act to manage risk by containment, by risk assessment, by insurance and by portfolios. Jack Welch was a good example here in his leadership of GE.

- **Egalitarians** have strong group loyalties but little respect for externally imposed rules, other than those imposed by nature. Group decisions about risks are arrived at democratically, and leaders rule by force of personality and persuasion. Risk is shared, and leadership is both about transactions and about collective transformations. We think that President Bill Clinton was a good example of this kind of leadership.

- **Fatalists** have minimum control over their own lives. They belong to no groups that are responsible for the decisions that rule their lives. They are non unionized, outcasts, on the margins of society. They are resigned to their fate and they see no point in attempting to change it. Risk is ignored, and leadership here can become self-destructive**. (It is difficult to think of an example here, because people like this do not become leaders. But some leaders do end up in this position, having failed to adapt, and just wait for the end.)

Adams (1995) went further to understand individual human behaviour in relationship to four elements of behaviour:

1. the recognizable propensity of individuals to take risks

2. the expectation or lure of rewards from risktaking

3. the perceived dangers arising from actions

4. expectations of accidents, i.e. the occurrence of danger

** Clearly, approaches to risk will differ among these four rationalities. In relation to the possibility of severe flood from global warming and more dry areas, the individualists will be risk seekers(sell water equipment);the hierarchists will seek to control risk (build national irrigation systems); the egalitarians will seek to share it within their groups and perhaps more widely (communal wells); the fatalists will accept the desert when it comes. Adams argued that individuals mediate these four elements by balancing behaviours. So a given preference for risks (see Chapter 2, Trait Theory), coupled with 'increased safety', can lead to compensating behaviours to take higher risks. And leaders, apart from the fatalists, will take higher personal, business and financial risks if they believe that their portfolio of investments or government regulators provide more safety. Some proposition like this underlies the argument that limited liability for shareholders is a moral hazard. The idea of risk compensation, where higher risks are taken as perceived dangers reduce and accidents reduce, leading to higher rewards, seems intuitively appealing – as indeed does its reverse, lower risks with lower rewards in the face of higher danger and more accidents.

Organizational Risk Management

The SWOT analysis, strategic positioning via the Boston Growth share matrix and strategic portfolio selection, including alliances, are examples of strategic risk management. It was found that markets could be viewed as establishing a relationship between risk and return, such that more risky assets were priced lower than less risky ones. This implies that markets were seeking a higher rate of return from more risky assets. Leaders should understand their own risk preferences and work at establishing the risk stance of their organization

Social and cultural context: Hofstedt (1980) included this variable in his characterization of national cultures (see Chapter 5). He characterized national culture along four dimensions, one of which was the degree of uncertainty avoidance – the degree to which members in a society feel uncomfortable in uncertain situations and seek to avoid them(by believing in absolute truths, the attainment of expertise, providing stability, establishing more formal rules and rejecting deviant ideas and behaviours). Ina major cross national project it was found that high manifestation to uncertainty avoidance was associated with enhancing outstanding leadership in some countries but quite the reverse in others. Comparison between Germany (high uncertainty avoidance) and the UK and Ireland (both low uncertainty avoidance). Hence organizations across the world in different cultures are unlikely to follow the more universal prescriptions of institutional risk management. We would expect firms from high uncertainty avoidance countries to be more hierarchist and those from low uncertainty avoidance countries to be more entrepreneurial. The leader of the organization that must take risks is in a bind, because some of the most serious risks are not calculable. It becomes a matter of judgment, which is why the idea of risk stance (as a view of leader personality) becomes critical.

The Risk Society: (public arenas of risk)

The consequence of modernism, with its thesis of progress, is to add to both natural and manmade hazards a series of constructed risks that are beyond experience, unlimited in time (thus affecting future generations) and unlimited by national boundaries. i.e. Chernobyl.

Risk Society is the distribution of *bads*; is individualised (Lash and Wyn; Beck, 1992: 3)

Leadership in a risk society: Reflexivity

The call for reflexivity in relation to risk inside and outside the organization means that the leadership task has to operate at the three levels of private, organization and public, both individually and collectively. Here the requirement is for leaders to 'step out' of business worlds and to understand how differences in the wider society will lead to the sharpest debates at the organizational and private levels. These leaders must understand that it is at these levels that evidence for and against any point of view is a matter of social construction and not a 'matter of fact'. Levels of attention: Leaders of organizations must take on both inter organizational and extra organizational roles and be prepared to engage with critical public debate about the science and technology in use or being proposed. What is required of leaders is the continuous process of seeking information, dialogue and understanding so that policy judgments embrace both the wider social risks and the intra organizational risks.

Learning Summary: Chapter 13

- While risk decisions are understood in terms of Type I and Type II errors, leaders have the responsibility for the Type III problem; that is, the task of framing decisions. Leaders must interpret external and internal environments in order to frame and put boundaries around decisions.

- Leaders have to ensure that adequate risk management processes are in place. These risk management processes should include attention to protection against the consequences, as well as seeking exposure to risks consonant with the growth and development of the organization.

- Leaders must take some care to ensure that the apparent reduction of risk in the overall organizations does not lead to exposure to increasing risk in order to retain a constant propensity to take risks.

- Leaders must be clear about their personal propensity to take, or appetite for risk, and that of their organization and its owners.

- Leaders may be observed as taking up any or all of the four stances of risk: individualist; hierarchist; egalitarian or fatalist. These shape the risk policy of organizations.

- It has been argued that leaders should recognize that not only do their organizations manage risks in relation to environment, but that these same organizations create and increase risks for the external environment.

- The interplay of environmental or societal risk and organizational risks means that leaders must be engaged in the public debates about risk and its management in order to ensure that societies do not make policy choices that do more harm than good.

- This latter point will require leaders to have high standards of ethical engagement and exposure to public debate, for the societal conceptions of risk require leaders to become involved in political processes for the good of the society and that of their organization.

14

A Critical Look at Leadership

Learning Objectives

- The ideological contexts of leadership theory;
- National and transnational ideological leadership issues;
- The idea of leaders as agents of others in the corporation;
- Three critiques of functional leadership: service, institutionalization and privilege;
- How the critiques move from a functional stance to a social constructionist stance;
- Three models of leader formation: an innate quality, innate qualities assisted by action reflection and theory building (which is where this course lies), and design and build.

We shall argue that three critiques – of mastery, of institutionalization and of taken-for-grantedness - let us see how leadership and leader formation are outcomes of the social and political context of organizations, as well as of psychology and personality. Leadership has been a high profile issue for orgs for centuries.

De Monthoux was keen to demonstrate how difficult it was to change orgs and when you do how quickly they settle into stable patterns. He implied that structure and order are enemies of innovation – hence some level of instability is necessary in orgs.

Dixon demonstrates how military structures can create high levels of dependence into which people with high dependent needs fit themselves. When such persons reach very senior positions, all is well until they have to act in battle as the decision-makers. At this point they have a tendency to become disabled and incompetent.

It seems that leadership of economic enterprises has become as rewarding as becoming a pop star. Certainly the boss's share of the enterprise income has risen. Yet it seems that job security has decreased for everyone. Perhaps risk and reward are related, but it does seem that the powerful managers can extract much higher rewards for the work they do and the risks they bear. Not much of the increased income appears to trickle down to the poor.

A new transnational order? - Economics, entertainment, sport and religion are aspects of globalization. But it is the case that the global reach and power of multinational enterprises has created – and is continuing to create – a new transnational economic order, substantially independent from national governments. In effect this new transnational economic order reflects the distribution of wealth that exists within the developed, developing and underdeveloped countries, with the very rich and the very poor inhabiting different spaces.

Can national leaders make rational economic choices? National leaders are major actors in this turbulent field. They are faced with five broad choices of economic policy, all of them ideological:

- To move towards laissez-faire. It is the case that no country or trading community either practices or wishes to practice laissez-faire capitalism, but the rise of neoliberalism is a move in that direction.

- To sustain social democracy via the middle way of a mixed economy of public and private provision. This includes the notion of a third way (see for example Dworkin, 2000), a new communitarianism.

- To reinstate democratic socialism, but this had failed very badly. In those countries that were socialized, privatization has been adopted together with other liberalization policies.

- To pursue state centralism of left or right (still surprisingly popular).

- To explore how ecological conservation can be the basis of a new order. This is the most puzzling and unknown course of action.

Leaders as agents in the corporation?

The corporate world of market capitalism (and late modernity) justifies itself and its behavior in relation to the maximization of shareholders wealth and contribution to global or national wealth. Hence a corporate CEO could logically take up the bounded and satisfying role of agent in relation to the principal (the shareholders). The CEO may be viewed as a 'contracted' agent of the principal. Indeed the literature of executive compensation is full of schemes designed to address the task of aligning the interests of the CEO as agent with that of the shareholders as principal. One way was to enlist the agent as a fellow principal by giving rewards to the CEO in shares. Another was to evaluate and reward the agent on the basis of performance (increase in market value) of the principal's shares in relation to that of either all company shares or of a selected comparison group. Most studies show that motivating the CEO as agents demonstrated that there are serious problems – most serious was the process of market valuation and timescale of consequences of the agent's action.

The CEO as agent is faced with multiple principals, the shareholders and directors and financial intermediaries as highly informed shareholders. Agent cannot serve so many potentially conflicting masters; the CEO may have a policy for action and outcomes that may suit some principals and not others.

We suggest that the CEO as agent is both a follower in relation to principals and perhaps a leader in organizing the task of serving the interests of the principals. But it has been argued that the interests of the agent and the principals necessarily diverge. This happens because, while the agent is working for the greater good of the principal, he is also (in this particular mindset) pursuing his self-interest (as a mirror of the self-interest of the principals). When the agent has expertise, knowledge and skills that the principals lack, then the temptation to exploit them exists. This conflict leads to what is described as a **moral hazard**, for the agent may not uniquely serve himself the principals but also serve herself as well (or better). The CEO as agent has become a team player, a creator of teams, in order that the very complexities and ambiguities of corporate work are addressed by interactive and parallel processing rather than by hierarchical or serial processing. In one sense, however, the reality of the 'team' does not change, for it is still the servant of the principals.

Three Critiques of Leadership- The first of these is presented by the ideas of servant leadership, the second comes from institutional theory, and the third from critical social theory.

1. **From Master to Servant** - The servanthood leadership theory exists in many religions. It seeks a radical equality of persons by requiring all to be servants for some good greater than the individuals' satisfaction or the wealth of shareholders. It centers actors upon the service of greater goods, e.g. the pursuit of justice, truth and peace, the removal of poverty, service to God and to others before gains for the self and, equally importantly, sharing of gifts and material goods across all places. It is in this that servanthood is the most radical critique of wealth generating leadership. The **counter critique** of servant hood is that it is hopelessly idealistic and does not reflect human aspirations, and while it may be suitable for actors in some voluntary organizations, the economic machine could not run with such principles, as they lack the wealth generating motivations.

2. **Institutionalizing Leadership** - modern organization is subject to environmental, technological and economic changes, and organizations might be better seen as political constitutions. If one views the firm from a constitutional perspective the modern firm must be seen as an institutional arrangement that has emerged in order to protect the owners, shareholders and principals as a group against the interest of individual members of this group, and to protect its long-term interests against its more short-term interests.'

3. **A critical account of Leadership** - The more radical critique of leadership is rooted in the attention of critical theory to the issues of power and its exercise (Alvesson and Willmott, 1992). This attention is not so much on the obvious process of commanding action, output and achievement and the unequal distribution of earned surpluses as rewards, but more on the power that is exercised in subtle and hidden ways and maintains the

legitimacy of the political constitution of Selznick in the form it does.

From Functional to Social Constructionism - It has been argued that leadership is a process of seduction to draw people into commitment to the corporation or organization. The role of organizational leaders and followers in the process of degradation are of course unconscious, but from a critical stance it is both forgivable and regrettable.

Can leaders control discourse? Part of the way in which discourse of organizational life is controlled is by distorted communication, both with and without conscious intent.

The formation of leaders – A social construction? How then do persons become leaders? Three common positions about formation are:

1. Leadership is innate and can be formed only on the job (so only other leaders can act as mentors). (Trait theory – which leaders are born and need to learn how- little evidence to sustain this theory).

2. Leadership can be assisted by a variety of action, reflection and contextual theory building processes. – Most research concentrated at this approach. Little consensus about how leaders become effective. The cognitive school offers the route of leader formation via process of loops of action, reflection, reconstructing, new designs for action and new experience. This approach presents a high ideal and considerable ethical content but does not engage with the critique from power and other discourses discussed in the module. An element of this second approach is of the leader as a kind of organizational therapist, in touch with the emotional life of himself and of the organization. Addressing emotions generates, it is said, the creative flow of unblocked activity.

3. Leaders can be designed and built. – Human engineering. Lacks evidence may be an ambition of organizational developers, trainers, teachers, and leaders themselves. Rests upon the positivist and functionalist approach.

Learning Summary: Chapter 14

- Understandings of leadership are caught up in ideologies. For example, the concept of strategy is drawn from the ideas of military leadership. You have your own ideology and will read the module from that stance.

- Much of the leadership theory and constructs used to explain them are drawn from western studies embedded in western cultures. There has been a regrettable tendency for these studies to be taught globally as though they fit all other societies and organizations.

- The rational constructs of leadership are themselves products of social constructions of theories and ideas. Mostly, the construct leader carries connotations of goodness, of being a good thing, but from other constructions, leaders are seen as the focus of oppression.

- Corporate leaders may see themselves as the servants or agent of the shareholders, and be so viewed in return. However, the different constructions of others would require the corporate leader to take on some much wider notions of agency, to government, to professions such as accounting and auditing, to employees and suppliers and customers.

- Three critiques of leadership underscore these learning points. The first two were a possible shift from master to servant and a process of institutionalizing leadership. The third sets out to give a critical account in demonstrating how leadership theory is complicit in the extant power structures, whether global, national or corporate. Further, these theories and constructs privilege leaders in relation to other actors.

- It is argued that the functional leadership theories are a process of seduction of others into compliance.

- The question of whether leaders can control discourses or whether the discourses control the leaders is central to a critical consideration of leadership.

- It is argued that leaders are formed in processes of social construction, for example, the functionalist approach claims that leaders can be designed and built, and also claims that leaders can only be formed by learning on the job. This would make leaders unreflective absorbers of what they are told or experience.

- There is a connection between critical approach to leadership and the reflexiveness discussed in Chapter 13. This is to encourage you to reconsider your own stance towards knowledge in general and to knowledge about leadership in particular.

Leadership is...

- a **process**...
- that involves **influence**,
- that is carried out in a **group** context,
- and that aims to achieve a **common goal**.

15

The Way Forward: Learning and Application of The Knowledge Of Leadership

Learning Objectives

- List the themes that were meaningful to you through the course of this study of leadership;

- Describe systems by which organizations learn;

- Describe how those systems can be employed to develop the leadership function within your own organization;

- List the five steps involved in managing your own leadership development process;

- Combine each of those steps into a leadership development plan that can be used to develop your own leadership effectiveness.

1: Learning About Leadership. Top leaders, it appears, tend to be very careful to listen to a range of views and relatively slow to come to a view. It seems that judgment is more important for them as it forms the context within which decisions can be made.

2: Trait Theory of Leadership. Trait theory addresses leadership from the viewpoint that leadership is driven by the individual's *characteristics*.

3: Behavior Theory of Leadership. The *actions* of the leader are the focus of the behavior theory of leadership.

4: Transformational Theory of Leadership. Transformational leadership shifts the focus of the leadership process from the leader to *the process that occurs between the leader and the follower.*

5: Leadership: A Cultural Construction? As with societies, organizations have cultures, and within these cultures, subcultures. Cultures influence 'how we do things around here', so culture needs to be considered as a portion of the leadership equation.

6: Gender and Leadership. One of the most striking workplace changes of the last century has been the proportion of women who have entered the world of work, including positions of leadership. Although there is still a glass ceiling, the changing needs of flatter and more flexible organizations operating in negotiated networks have led to the suggestion that the stereotypical female capabilities (interpersonal skills, communication, empathy, collaboration, conflict handling and negotiation) might be of more use than those of the male (competitiveness, aggression, strategic planning and winning) and lead to higher effectiveness.

7: Developing Ethical Behavior in Leaders. Ethics, doing the right thing, is good for business as well as for the organization's stakeholders. But being within the limits of the law does not necessarily constitute ethical behavior.

8: Leading Individuals and Teams. The job of the leader is to ensure that the follower is successful.

9: Leadership across the Larger Organization. Providing leadership across the total organization is the most complex and challenging of all leadership situations. Those whom the leader wishes to influence may not be within the leader's direct reporting structure or may report only very indirectly, layers down within the organization. Therefore, the leader is likely to need to employ leadership behaviors identified by Kouzes and Posner among successful leaders: *modeling the way, inspiring a shared vision, challenging the process, enabling others to act,* and *encouraging the heart.*

10: Leadership Development in a Fast Changing World. Leadership development programs have been readily available for 40 years. And yet, today, most organizations report that they will not have the required numbers or types of leaders available to meet future needs. A major cause of this shortfall may be that leaders are today confronted with different leadership situations: a much more complex world, a more sophisticated and demanding workforce, work increasingly accomplished through teams, the need for a transformational leadership approach, and constantly changing jobs. Therefore we can no longer focus on developing leaders in organizations. Rather, we must develop the leadership function through policies, systems and strategic review.

11: The Development Leadership: Tools and Practices. If organizations are to develop their leadership function, it is incumbent on them to employ the most effective tools, methods and systems, based on sound learning theory.

12. Strategic Leadership. It is easy to think of a leader in the role of hero, instantly assessing the nature of a crisis and rallying and directing followers to respond. The reality is that almost every organization must plan and execute in a much longer timeframe in order to survive and indeed prosper. Strategic leadership is the key role in this process. A number of models of strategy development are available, but they all require the elements of *configuring*, *facilitating*, *delivering*, *evaluating* and *changing*.

13: Leadership and Risk. Interwoven in the process of leadership is the matter of understanding and managing risk. Few decisions can be taken without incurring some degree of risk. But there is also risk in deciding to do nothing, or not deciding at all.

14: A Critical Look at Leadership. In spite of the vast body of research and writing about leadership, understanding of its formation is still quite limited. One reason may be the transnationalism in which the leader functions. Making economic choices for organizations that at first seem logical and in the best traditions of capitalism may soon run into a vast array of unpredictable influences, the context, values, organizations and traditions of other entities influenced by such choices. Consequently, the leader may have only limited scope actually to lead, perhaps being primarily a product of society, the organization and the context.

Organizational Learning Systems

The most valuable part of any organization is the combined knowledge of its employees. Efforts at managing organizational learning have typically been modeled after the traditional library: people who have knowledge record it and place it in the library. Unfortunately, that system doesn't work. There are at least three reasons for this:

- **First**, it is very difficult to get busy individuals to record their learning faithfully and consistently.

- **Second**, knowledge that *is* recorded is explicit.

- **Finally**, most organizational learning libraries are limited for lack of resources or support;

Table 15.1   Dixon's organisational learning systems

Learning system	Application	Example
Near transfer	Transferring explicit knowledge from one situation to a similar situation	One shift at a manufacturing site realised improvements with different machine settings and shared that knowledge with other shifts
Far transfer	Transferring tacit knowledge of non-routine tasks across the organisation	A new manufacturing injection moulding operation in Malaysia is able to decrease changeover times by studying the organisational 'best practices' of a Brazilian sister plant
Serial transfer	Transferring tacit and explicit knowledge of a team to the next time a team does the task in a different setting	Each time a fire department returns from a major fire, it reviews the event to improve future practices
Strategic transfer	Transferring tacit and explicit knowledge from across the organisation to a specific, infrequent task or problem	As a retail organisation plans to open a new operation in South America, experts from throughout the company attend a 2-day workshop to advise the team responsible for the new task
Expert transfer	Transferring explicit and tacit knowledge from technical experts to individuals or teams in need of that knowledge	An international logistics organisation maintains a list of individuals who have been involved in the opening of new warehouses so that any team, when opening a new warehouse, can contact these experts for advice and input

Each organization will develop its own, unique system, meeting its aspirations and philosophy and working within the organization's culture. To implement the five learning systems shown above, one can answer questions such as:

- How effective is the graduate intake program?

- Are the leadership competencies still relevant?

- What are the outcomes of leadership development training programs?

- What developmental assignments are most effective in developing tomorrow's executives?

- How well is the succession planning process meeting its purpose?

- How do the followers view organizational leadership?

Principles to guide leaders:

1. **Gather a clear picture of your leadership and keep it current:** Feedback is the most important component of any skill development process. The feedback process really has two stages: gaining that feedback, and then understanding and accepting it so that we may take meaning from it. Leaders can also ask those most in the know, their followers, for feedback. Leaders must not only actively seek feedback on an ongoing basis; they must also understand and accept it.

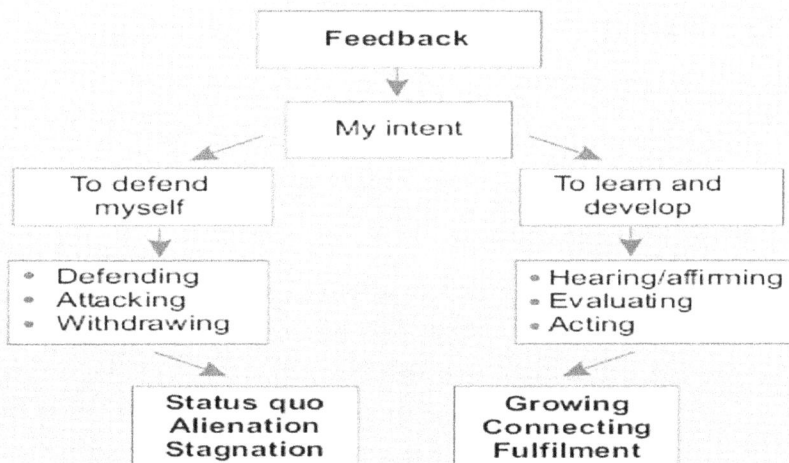

Feedback

↓

My intent

To defend myself → To learn and develop

- Defending
- Attacking
- Withdrawing

- Hearing/affirming
- Evaluating
- Acting

Status quo
Alienation
Stagnation

Growing
Connecting
Fulfilment

Ensuring feedback results in growth

2. **Develop a plan to address any current issues.** It is very easy to think of development planning as a process supporting career planning.

3. **Develop a realistic plan to develop for future challenges.** As current issues are addressed, then it is appropriate to began looking to the future. Aspect of development planning also needs to involve quality-of-life considerations: the requirements of families, the willingness to relocate geographically, leisure time and community involvements and much more. Perhaps a final input needs to be a good measure of realism: what aspirations, given all of the feedback, self-analysis, environmental understanding as so on, can be realistically fulfilled? There is somewhat of an art to goal setting. Goals that do not challenge do not lead to fulfillment. Goals that are unattainable lead only to disappointment. But stretch goals, goals that are challenging, yet realistic, are the ones that lead to personal fulfillment and organizational success.

4. **Self lead, make the plans happen.** Commitment is not enough. It works best when the leader institutes concrete, almost mechanical processes that remind, reinforce and keep the process on course. Some examples include the following:

   • Developmental goals with task goals in the annual performance planning process, with equal levels of accountability.

   • A development agenda in periodic meetings with the leader's manager.

   • Placing reminders at future dates in a time management system.

   • Posting development objectives above the desk.

   • Developing a coaching or mentoring relationship with another person to support development goals.

   • Scheduling 'thinking' time each week to review progress.

5. **View leadership development as a continuing process**: periodically evaluate and renew. leadership development is not a destination. It is a journey. For successful leaders it will never end. There is always more to learn. Situations will always change. Skills will always need to be honed and developed.

New ways of doing, thinking and being will be required. In this fast changing world there is no choice if we are not only to survive, but indeed, to thrive. Effective leadership development occurs year in and year out. It is a rich combination of work assignments, short courses, personal reading, being mentored, mentoring others, web based learning, degree programs, membership of professional organizations, community projects and more. It is never the same for any two people. But what is the same is that it is an ongoing professional habit, a process pursued throughout the leader's professional life.

*View leadership development
as a continuing process.*

16

Leadership Theories

Studies in leadership increased considerably as early twentieth century emerged. Early leadership theories focused on what qualities distinguished between leaders and followers, while subsequent theories looked at other variables such as situational factors and skill levels. While various leadership theories have emerged, most can be classified as one of eight major types:

1. "Great Man" Theories:

Great man theories assume that the capacity for leadership is inherent – that great leaders are born; not made. These theories often portray great leaders as heroic, mythic and destined to rise to leadership when needed. The term "Great Man" became popular at the time since leadership was thought of primarily as a male quality, especially in terms of military leadership. Learn more about the great man theory of leadership.

Have you ever heard the phrase, "Great leaders are born, not made."? This quote sums up the basic tenet of the great man theory of leadership, which suggests that the capacity for leadership is inborn. According to this theory, you're either a natural born leader or you're not.

The term "Great Man" was used because, at the time, leadership was thought of primarily as a male quality, especially in terms of military leadership.

History of the Great Man Theory of Leadership

The great man theory of leadership became popular during the 19th-century. The mythology behind some of the world's most famous leaders such as Abraham Lincoln, Julius Caesar, Mahatma Gandhi, and Alexander the Great helped contribute to the notion that great leaders are born and not made. In many examples, it seems as if the right man for the job seems to emerge almost magically to take control of a situation and lead a group of people into safety or success.

Historian Thomas Carlyle also had a major influence on this theory of leadership, at one point stating that, "The history of the world is but the biography of great men." According to Carlyle, effective leaders are those gifted with divine inspiration and the right characteristics.

Some of the earliest research on leadership looked at people who were already successful leaders. These individuals often included aristocratic rulers who achieved their position through birthright. Because people of a lesser social status had fewer opportunities to practice and achieve leadership roles, it contributed to the idea that leadership is an inherent ability.

Even today, people often describe prominent leaders as having the right qualities or personality for the position, implying that inherent characteristics are what make these people effective leaders.

Arguments against the Great Man Theory of Leadership

Sociologist Herbert Spencer suggested that the leaders were products of the society in which they lived. In *The Study of Sociology*, Spencer wrote, "you must admit that the genesis of a great man depends on the long series of complex influences which has produced the race in which he appears, and the social state into which that race has slowly grown.... Before he can remake his society, his society must make him."

References:

Carlyle, T. (1888). On Heroes, Hero-Worship and the Heroic in History, Fredrick A. Stokes & Brother, New York.

Hirsch, E.D. (2002). The New Dictionary of Cultural Literacy (Third Edition). Houghton Mifflin Company, Boston.

Spencer, H. (1896). The Study of Sociology, Appleton, New York.

Straker, D. Great man theory. Changing Minds. Found online at http://changingminds. org/disciplines/leadership/theories/great_man_theory.htm

Suggested Reading

- Branches of Psychology

- Quotes: Leadership Motivation
- Secrets of Leadership Success

Related Articles

- Leadership Theories - Eight Major Leadership Theories
- Popular Leadership Models - Leadership
- Secrets of Leadership Success
- Charismatic Leadership
- Leadership Quotes

2. Trait Theories:

Similar in some ways to "Great Man" theories, trait theories assume that people inherit certain qualities and traits that make them better suited to leadership. Trait theories often identify particular personality or behavioral characteristics shared by leaders. If particular traits are key features of leadership, then how do we explain people who possess those qualities but are not leaders? This question is one of the difficulties in using trait theories to explain leadership.

The trait approach to personality is one of the major theoretical areas in the study of personality. The trait theory suggests that individual personalities are composed broad dispositions. Consider how you would describe the personality of a close friend. Chances are that you would list a number of traits, such as *outgoing*, *kind* and *even-tempered*. A trait can be thought of as a relatively stable characteristic that causes individuals to behave in certain ways.

Unlike many other theories of personality, such as psychoanalytic or humanistic theories, the trait approach to personality is focused on differences between individuals. The combination and interaction of various traits forms a personality that is unique to each individual. Trait theory is focused on identifying and measuring these individual personality characteristics.

Gordon Allport's Trait Theory

In 1936, psychologist Gordon Allport found that one English-language dictionary alone contained more than 4,000 words describing different personality traits.[1] He categorized these traits into three levels:

- **Cardinal Traits:** Traits that dominate an individual's whole life, often to the point that the person becomes known specifically for these traits. People with such personalities often become so known for these traits that their names are often synonymous with these qualities. Consider the origin and meaning of the following descriptive terms: Freudian, Machiavellian, narcissism, Don Juan, Christ-like, etc. Allport suggested that cardinal traits are rare and tend to develop later in life.[2]

- **Central Traits:** These are the general characteristics that form the basic foundations of personality. These central traits, while not as dominating as cardinal traits, are the major characteristics you might use to describe another person. Terms such as *intelligent, honest, shy* and *anxious* are considered central traits.

- **Secondary Traits:** These are the traits that are sometimes related to attitudes or preferences and often appear only in certain situations or under specific circumstances. Some examples would be getting anxious when speaking to a group or impatient while waiting in line.

Raymond Cattell's Sixteen Personality Factor Questionnaire

Trait theorist Raymond Cattell reduced the number of main personality traits from Allport's initial list of over 4,000 down to 171, mostly by eliminating uncommon traits and combining common characteristics. Next, Cattell rated a large sample of individuals for these 171 different traits. Then, using a statistical technique known as factor analysis, he identified closely related terms and eventually reduced his list to just 16 key personality traits. According to Cattell, these 16 traits are the source of all human personality. He also developed one of the most widely used personality assessments known as the Sixteen Personality Factor Questionnaire (16PF).

Eysenck's Three Dimensions of Personality

British psychologist Hans Eysenck developed a model of personality based upon just three universal trails:

1. Introversion/Extraversion:

Introversion involves directing attention on inner experiences, while extraversion relates to focusing attention outward on other people and the environment. So, a person high in introversion might be quiet and reserved, while an individual high in extraversion might be sociable and outgoing.

2. Neuroticism/Emotional Stability:

This dimension of Eysenck's trait theory is related to moodiness versus even-temperedness. Neuroticism refers to an individual's tendency to become upset or emotional, while stability refers to the tendency to remain emotionally constant.

3. Psychoticism:

Later, after studying individuals suffering from mental illness, Eysenck added a personality dimension he called psychoticism to his trait theory. Individuals who are high on this trait tend to have difficulty dealing with reality and may be antisocial, hostile, non-empathetic and manipulative.[4]

The Five-Factor Theory of Personality

Both Cattell's and Eysenck's theory have been the subject of considerable research, which has led some theorists to believe that Cattell focused on too many traits, while Eysenck focused on too few. As a result, a new trait theory often referred to as the "Big Five" theory emerged. This five-factor model of personality represents five core traits that interact to form human personality.[5] While researchers often disagree about the exact labels for each dimension, the following are described most commonly:

1. Extraversion

2. Agreeableness

3. Conscientiousness

4. Neuroticism

5. Openness

Assessing the Trait Approach to Personality

While most agree that people can be described based upon their personality traits, theorists continue to debate the number of basic traits that make up human personality. While trait theory has objectivity that some personality theories lack (such as Freud's psychoanalytic theory), it also has weaknesses. Some of the most common criticisms of trait theory center on the fact that traits are often poor predictors of behavior. While an individual may score high on assessments of a specific trait, he or she may not always behave that way in every situation. Another problem is that trait theories do not address how or why individual differences in personality develop or emerge.

References:

Allport, G.W. & Odbert, H.S. (1936). Trait-names: A psycho-lexical study. Psychological Monographs, 47(211).

Boeree, C.G. (2006). Gordon Allport. Personality Theories. Found online at http://webspace.ship.edu/cgboer/allport.html

Cattell, R.B. (1965). The scientific analysis of personality. Baltimore: Penguin Books.

Eysenck, H.J. (1992). Four ways five factors are not basic. Personality and Individual Differences, 13, 667-673.

McCrae, R.R., & Costa, P.T. (1997) Personality trait structure as a human universal. American Psychologist, 52, 509-516.

More Theories of Personality

- Big Five Personality Traits
- Theory of Neurotic Needs
- Psychogenic Needs

Suggested Reading

- Theories of Personality Development
- What is Personality Psychology?
- Personality - What Is Personality

Personality Theorists

- Gordon Allport
- Raymond Cattell
- Sigmund Freud

Related Articles

- Personality - What Is Personality
- Personality Development - Theories of Personality Development

3. Contingency Theories:

Contingency theories of leadership focus on particular variables related to the environment that might determine which particular style of leadership is best suited for the situation. According to this theory, no leadership style is best in all situations. Success depends upon a number of variables, including the leadership style, qualities of the followers and aspects of the situation.

4. Situational Theories:

Situational theories propose that leaders choose the best course of action based upon situational variables. Different styles of leadership may be more appropriate for certain types of decision-making.

5. Behavioral Theories:

Behavioral theories of leadership are based upon the belief that great leaders are made, not born. Rooted in behaviorism, this leadership theory focuses on the actions of leaders not on mental qualities or internal states. According to this theory, people can *learn* to become leaders through teaching and observation.

Question: What Is Behaviorism?

Give me a dozen healthy infants, well-formed, and my own specified world to bring them up in and I'll guarantee to take any one at random and train him to become any type of specialist I might select -- doctor, lawyer, artist, merchant-chief and, yes, even beggar-man and thief, regardless of his talents, penchants, tendencies, abilities, vocations, and race of his ancestors.

--John Watson, **Behaviorism**, 1930

Answer:

Behavioral psychology, also known as behaviorism, is a theory of learning based upon the idea that all behaviors are acquired through conditioning. Conditioning occurs through interaction with the environment. According to behaviorism, behavior can be studied in a systematic and observable manner with no consideration of internal mental states.

There are two major types of conditioning:

1. Classical conditioning is a technique used in behavioral training in which a naturally occurring stimulus is paired with a response. Next, a previously neutral stimulus is paired with the naturally occurring stimulus. Eventually, the previously neutral stimulus comes to evoke the response without the presence of the naturally occurring stimulus. The two elements are then known as the conditioned stimulus and the conditioned response.

2. Operant conditioning (sometimes referred to as instrumental conditioning) is a method of learning that occurs through rewards and punishments for behavior. Through operant conditioning, an association is made between a behavior and a consequence for that behavior.

Major Thinkers in Behaviorism

*   Ivan Pavlov

*   B. F. Skinner

*   Edward Thorndike

*   John B. Watson

*   Clark Hull

Important Events in Behaviorism

*   1863 - Ivan Sechenov's **Reflexes of the Brain** was published. Sechenov introduced the concept of inhibitory responses in the central nervous system.

*   1900 - Ivan Pavlov began studying the salivary response and other reflexes.

*   1913 - John Watson's *Psychology as a Behaviorist Views It* was published. The article outlined the many of the main points of behaviorism.

- 1920 - Watson and assistant Rosalie Rayner conducted the famous "Little Albert" experiment.

- 1943 - Clark Hull's *Principles of Behavior* was published.

- 1948 - B.F. Skinner published *Walden II* in which he described a utopian society founded upon behaviorist principles.

- 1959 - Noam Chomsky published his criticism of Skinner's behaviorism, "Review of Verbal Behavior."

- 1971 - B.F. Skinner published his book *Beyond Freedom and Dignity*, where he argues that free will is an illusion.

Criticisms of Behaviorism

- Many critics argue that behaviorism is a one-dimensional approach to behavior and behavioral theories do not account for free will and internal influences such as moods, thoughts and feelings.

- Behaviorism does not account for other types of learning, especially learning that occurs without the use of reinforcement and punishment.

- People and animals are able to adapt their behavior when new information is introduced, even if a previous behavior pattern has been established through reinforcement.

Strengths of Behaviorism

- Behaviorism is based upon observable behaviors, so it is easier to quantify and collect data and information when conducting research.

- Effective therapeutic techniques such as intensive behavioral intervention, behavior analysis, token economies and discrete trial training are all rooted in behaviorism. These approaches are often very useful in changing maladaptive or harmful behaviors in both children and adults.

Final Thoughts

While behaviorism is not as dominant today as it was during the middle of the 20th-century, it still remains an influential force in psychology. Outside of psychology, animal trainers, parents, teachers and many others make use of basic behavioral principles to help teach new behaviors and discourage unwanted behaviors.

More about Behaviorism

- Behavioral Psychology 101
- Intro to Classical Conditioning
- Intro to Operant Conditioning

Suggested Reading

- What Is Behavior Analysis?
- Schedules of Reinforcement

Suggested Reading

- John B. Watson Biography
- Ivan Pavlov Biography
- B. F. Skinner Biography

Related Articles

- Learning Study Guide - Psychology of Learning - Study Guide
- Behaviorism - What Is Behaviorism
- John Watson - Biography of John Watson
- Operant Conditioning - Introduction to Operant Conditioning
- Learning and Conditioning Quiz

6. Participative Theories:

Participative leadership theories suggest that the ideal leadership style is one that takes the input of others into account. These leaders encourage participation and contributions from group members and help group members feel more relevant and committed to the decision-making process. In participative theories, however, the leader retains the right to allow the input of others.

7. Management Theories:

Management theories, also known as transactional theories, focus on the role of supervision, organization and group performance. These theories base leadership on a system of rewards and punishments. Managerial theories are often used in business; when employees are successful, they are rewarded; when they fail, they are reprimanded or punished. Learn more about theories of transactional leadership.

Question: What Is Transactional Leadership?

Answer:

Transactional leadership, also known as managerial leadership, focuses on the role of supervision, organization and group performance. This theory of leadership was first described in by sociologist Max Weber, and further explored by Bernard M. Bass in the early 1980s.

Basic Assumptions of Transactional Leadership

- People perform their best when the chain of command is definite and clear.

- Workers are motivated by rewards and punishments.

- Obeying the instructions and commands of the leader is the primary goal of the followers.

- Subordinates need to be carefully monitored to ensure that expectations are met.

This theory bases leadership on a system of rewards and punishments. Transactional leadership is often used in business; when employees are successful, they are rewarded; when they fail, they are reprimanded or punished.

How Transactional Leadership Works

In transactional leadership, rewards and punishments are contingent upon the performance of the followers. The leader views the relationship between managers and subordinates as an exchange - you give me something for something in return. When subordinates perform well, they receive some type of reward. When they perform poorly, they will be punished in some way.

Rules, procedures and standards are essential in transactional leadership. Followers are not encouraged to be creative or to find new solutions to problems. Research has found that transactional leadership tends to be most effective in situations where problems are simple and clearly-defined.

While transactional leadership can be effective in some situations, it is generally considered an insufficient and may prevent both leaders an followers from achieving their full potential.

References:

Bass, B. M,(1985), Leadership and Performance, N.Y. Free Press.

Burns, J.M. (1978) Leadership. New York. Harper & Row

Leadership Styles

- Transformational Leadership
- Democratic Leadership
- Autocratic Leadership

More about Leadership

- Leadership Theories - Eight Major Leadership Theories
- Laissez-Faire Leadership
- Quiz - What's Your Leadership Style?

Suggested Reading

- Lewin's Leadership Styles - Three Major Leadership Styles
- Great Man Theories - Great Man Theories of Leadership
- Branches of Psychology

Related Articles

- Transformational Leadership - What Is Transformational Leadership
- Quiz - What's Your Leadership Style?
- Laissez-Faire Leadership - What Is Laissez-Faire Leadership
- Leadership Theories - Eight Major Leadership Theories
- Great Man Theories - Great Man Theories of Leadership

8. Relationship Theories:

Relationship theories, also known as transformational theories, focus upon the connections formed between leaders and followers. Transformational leaders motivate and inspire people by helping group members see the importance and higher good of the task. These leaders are focused on the performance of group members, but also want each person to fulfill his or her potential. Leaders with this style often have high ethical and moral standards.

Have you ever been in a group situation where someone took control of the situation by conveying a clear vision of the group's goals, a marked passion for the work and an ability to make the rest of the group feel recharged and energized? This person just might be what is called a transformational leader.

Transformational leadership is a type of leadership style that leads to positive changes in those who follow. Transformational leaders are generally energetic, enthusiastic and passionate. Not only are these leaders concerned and involved in the process; they are also focused on helping every member of the group succeed as well.

The History of Transformational Leadership

The concept of transformational leadership was initially introduced by leadership expert and presidential biographer James MacGregor Burns.[1] According to Burns, transformational leadership can be seen when "leaders and followers make each other to advance to a higher level of moral and motivation." Through the strength of their vision and personality, transformational leaders are able to inspire followers to change expectations, perceptions and motivations to work towards common goals.

Later, researcher Bernard M. Bass expanded upon Burns original ideas to develop what is today referred to as Bass' Transformational Leadership Theory.[2] According to Bass, transformational leadership can be defined based on the impact that it has on followers. Transformational leaders, Bass suggested, garner trust, respect and admiration from their followers.

The Components of Transformational Leadership

Bass also suggested that there were four different components of transformational leadership.

1. **Intellectual Stimulation** – Transformational leaders not only challenge the status quo; they also encourage creativity among followers. The leader encourages followers to explore new ways of doing things and new opportunities to learn.

2. **Individualized Consideration** – Transformational leadership also involves offering support and encouragement to individual followers. In order to foster supportive relationships, transformational leaders keep lines of communication open so that followers feel free to share ideas and so that leaders can offer direct recognition of each follower's unique contributions.

3. **Inspirational Motivation** – Transformational leaders have a clear vision that they are able to articulate to followers. These leaders are also able to help followers experience the same passion and motivation to fulfill these goals.

4. **Idealized Influence** – The transformational leaders serves as a role model for followers. Because followers trust and respect the leader, they emulate the leader and internalize his or her ideals.

References

Burns, J.M. (1978). Leadership. N.Y: Harper and Raw.

Bass,B. M,(1985). Leadership and Performance. N. Y,: Free Press.

Riggio, R.E. (2009, March 24). Are you a transformational leader. Psychology Today. Found online at http://blogs.psychologytoday.com/blog/cutting-edge-leadership/200903/are-you-transformational-leader

More About Leadership

- Leadership Theories - Eight Major Leadership Theories
- Lewin's Leadership Styles - Three Major Leadership Styles
- Quiz - What's Your Leadership Style?

Related Articles

- Lead the Team: How to be the Person Others Follow: Leadership Success Secre...

- <u>Charismatic Leadership</u>

- <u>Transactional Leadership - What Is Transactional Leadership</u>

- <u>5 Keys to Leadership - How to Become a Leader</u>

- <u>Quiz - What's Your Leadership Style?</u>

In 1939, a group of researchers led by psychologist Kurt Lewin set out to identify different styles of leadership. While further research has identified more specific types of leadership, this early study was very influential and established three major leadership styles. In the study, groups of schoolchildren were assigned to one of three groups with an authoritarian, democratic or laissez-fair leader. The children were then led in an arts and crafts project. Researchers then observed the behavior of children in response to the different styles of leadership.

Authoritarian Leadership (Autocratic)

Authoritarian leaders, also known as autocratic leaders, provide clear expectations for what needs to be done, when it should be done, and how it should be done. There is also a clear division between the leader and the followers. Authoritarian leaders make decisions independently with little or no input from the rest of the group.

Researchers found that decision-making was less creative under authoritarian leadership. Lewin also found that it is more difficult to move from an authoritarian style to a democratic style than vice versa. Abuse of this style is usually viewed as controlling, bossy, and dictatorial.

Authoritarian leadership is best applied to situations where there is little time for group decision-making or where the leader is the most knowledgeable member of the group.

Participative Leadership (Democratic)

Lewin's study found that participative leadership, also known as democratic leadership, is generally the most effective leadership style. Democratic leaders offer guidance to group members, but they also participate in the group and allow input from other group members. In

Lewin's study, children in this group were less productive than the members of the authoritarian group, but their contributions were of a much higher quality.

Participative leaders encourage group members to participate, but retain the final say over the decision-making process. Group members feel engaged in the process and are more motivated and creative.

Delegative (Laissez-Faire) Leadership

Researchers found that children under delegative leadership, also known as laissez-fair leadership, were the least productive of all three groups. The children in this group also made more demands on the leader, showed little cooperation and were unable to work independently.

Delegative leaders offer little or no guidance to group members and leave decision-making up to group members. While this style can be effective in situations where group members are highly qualified in an area of expertise, it often leads to poorly defined roles and a lack of motivation.

Reference:

Lewin, K., Lippit, R. and White, R.K. (1939). Patterns of aggressive behavior in experimentally created social climates. *Journal of Social Psychology, 10,* 271-301

Question: What Is Autocratic Leadership?

Answer: Autocratic leadership, also known as authoritarian leadership, is a leadership style characterized by individual control over all decisions and little input from group members. Autocratic leaders typically make choices based on their own ideas and judgments and rarely accept advice from followers. Autocratic leadership involves absolute, authoritarian control over a group.

Characteristics of Autocratic Leadership

Some of the primary characteristics of autocratic leadership include:

- Little or no input from group members
- Leaders make the decisions
- Group leaders dictate all the work methods and processes
- Group members are rarely trusted with decisions or important tasks

Benefits of Autocratic Leadership

Autocratic leadership can be beneficial in some instances, such as when decisions need to be made quickly without consulting with a large group of people. Some projects require strong leadership in order to get things accomplished quickly and efficiently.

Have you ever worked with a group of students or co-workers on a project that got derailed by poor organization, a lack of leadership and an inability to set deadlines? If so, chances are that your grade or job performance suffered as a result. In such situations, a strong leader who utilizes an autocratic style can take charge of the group, assign tasks to different members and establish solid deadlines for projects to be finished.

In situations that are particularly stressful, such as during military conflicts, group members may actually prefer an autocratic style. It allows members of the group to focus on performing specific tasks without worrying about making complex decisions. This also allows group members to become highly skilled at performing certain duties, which can be beneficial to the group.

Downsides of Autocratic Leadership

While autocratic leadership can be beneficial at times, there are also many instances where this leadership style can be problematic. People who abuse an autocratic leadership style are often viewed as bossy, controlling and dictatorial, which can lead to resentment among group members.

Because autocratic leaders make decisions without consulting the group, people in the group may dislike that they are unable to contribute ideas. Researchers have also found that autocratic leadership leads to a lack of creative solutions to problems, which can ultimately hurt the performance of the group.

While autocratic leadership does have some potential pitfalls, leaders can learn to use elements of this style wisely. For example, an autocratic style can be used effectively in situations where the leader is the most knowledgeable member of the group or has access to information that other members of the group do not.

Question: What Is Democratic Leadership?

Answer: Democratic leadership, also known as participative leadership, is a type of leadership style in which members of the group take a more participative role in the decision-making process. Researchers have found that this learning style is usually one of the most effective and leaders to higher productivity, better contributions from group members and increased group morale.

Characteristics of Democratic Leadership

Some of the primary characteristics of democratic leadership include:

- Group members are encouraged to share ideas and opinions, even though the leader retains the final say over decisions.

- Members of the group feel more engaged in the process.

- Creativity is encouraged and rewarded.

Benefits of Democratic Leadership

Because group members are encouraged to share their thoughts, democratic leadership can leader to better ideas and more creative solutions to problems. Group members also feel more involved and committed to projects, making them more likely to care about the end results. Research on leadership styles has also show that democratic leadership leads to higher productivity among group members.

Downsides of Democratic Leadership

While democratic leadership has been described as the most effective leadership style, it does have some potential downsides. In situations where roles are unclear or time is of the essence, democratic leadership can lead to communication failures and uncompleted projects. In some cases, group members may not have the necessary knowledge or expertise to make quality contributions to the decision-making process.

Democratic leadership works best in situations where group members are skilled and eager to share their knowledge. It is also important to have plenty of time to allow people to contribute, develop a plan and then vote on the best course of action.

Question: What Is Laissez-Faire Leadership?

Answer: Laissez-faire leadership, also known as delegative leadership, is a type of leadership style in which leaders are hands-off and allow group members to make the decisions. Researchers have found that this is generally the leadership style that leads to the lowest productivity among group members.

Characteristics of Laissez-Faire Leadership

Laissez-faire leadership is characterized by:

- Very little guidance from leaders

- Complete freedom for followers to make decisions

- Leaders provide the tools and resources needed

- Group members are expected to solve problems on their own

Benefits of Laissez-Faire Leadership

Laissez-faire leadership can be effective in situations where group members are highly skilled, motivated and capable of working on their own. While the conventional term for this style is 'laissez-faire' and implies a completely hands-off approach, many leaders still remain open and available to group members for consultation and feedback.

Downsides of Laissez-Faire Leadership

Laissez-faire leadership is not ideal in situations where group members lack the knowledge or experience they need to complete tasks and make decisions. Some people are not good at setting their own deadlines, managing their own projects and solving problems on their own. In such situations, projects can go off-track and deadlines can be missed when team members do not get enough guidance or feedback from leaders.

Know when to speak, when to stay silent.

References

Allport, G.W. & Odbert, H.S. (1936). Trait-names: A psycho-lexical study. *Psychological Monographs, 47*(211).

Bass, B. M,(1985), *Leadership and Performance*, N.Y. Free Press.

Boeree, C.G. (2006). Gordon Allport. *Personality Theories*. Found online at http://webspace.ship.edu/cgboer/allport.html

Burns, J.M. (1978) *Leadership*. New York. Harper & Row

Carlyle, T. (1888). *On Heroes, Hero-Worship and the Heroic in History*, Fredrick A. Stokes & Brother, New York.

Cattell, R.B. (1965). *The Scientific Analysis of Personality*. Baltimore: Penguin Books.

Eysenck, H.J. (1992). Four ways five factors are not basic. *Personality and Individual Differences, 13*, 667-673.

Hirsch, E.D. (2002). *The New Dictionary of Cultural Literacy* (Third Edition). Houghton Mifflin Company, Boston.

Lewin, K., Lippit, R. and White, R.K. (1939). Patterns of aggressive behavior in experimentally created social climates. *Journal of Social Psychology, 10,* 271-301

McCrae, R.R., & Costa, P.T. (1997) Personality trait structure as a human universal. *American Psychologist, 52*, 509-516.

Moyer, Bill, JoAnn McAllister, Mary Lou Finley and Steve Soifer, (2001), *Doing Democracy: The MAP Model for Organizing Social Movements*, New Society Publishers: Gabriola Island, British Columbia

Riggio, R.E. (2009, March 24). *Are you a transformational leader?* Psychology Today. Found online at http://blogs.psychologytoday.com/blog/cutting-edge-leadership/200903/are-you-transformational-leader

Ritzer, George, (2000), *The McDonalization of Society*, New century ed., Pine Forge Press: Thousand Oaks, California

Spencer, H. (1896). *The Study of Sociology*, Appleton, New York.

Straker, D. *Great Man Theory. Changing Minds*. Found online at http://changingminds.org/disciplines/leadership/theories/great_man_theory.htm

Zunes, Steven, Lester Kurtz, Sarah Beth Asher, (1991), eds., *Nonviolent Social Movements: A Geographical Perspective*, Blackwell: University of San Francisco

Student Section

Leadership Theory
&
Social Change

LSC 806 – 23

This course examines Social Change globally from both macro and micro perspectives; both long and short term. There are several dimensions including individual change, institutional change, social movements, and nonviolence, and eternal change.

Professor:
Paratan Balloo, MBA, DPhil

O.A.S.I.S. Institute of Higher Learning

Omega Advanced Schools for Interdisciplinary Studies

This course considers the formal and informal aspects of leadership in organizations. Major theories of leadership will be considered, discussed, and investigated for application in to the structure, processes, and behavior of organized groups. The sympathetic and cybernetic aspects of leadership are considered in the context of process of social change.

Social Theory - **Social theories** are theoretical frameworks which are used to study and interpret social phenomena within a particular school of thought. An essential tool used by social scientists, theories relate to historical debates over the most valid and reliable methodologies (e.g. positivism and anti-positivism), as well as the primacy of either structure or agency. Certain social theories attempt to remain strictly scientific, descriptive, and objective. Conflict theories, by contrast, present ostensibly normative positions, and often critique the ideological aspects inherent in conventional, traditional thought.

OBJECTIVES

- At the end of this course students will be familiar with major theories of leadership and their application and practice within organizations.

- Leadership will be discussed in alternate contexts including non-governmental, political, and social.

- Students will be required to research for discussion leaders of social change globally identifying key aspects of approaches to social change.

EXPECTATIONS AND GRADING

- Complete developmental readings.

- Review and write notes on four of the major leadership theories.

- Refer to article by Daniel Goldman on "Leadership that Gets Results", supplement with other readings, and reproduce document with applications and practices of leadership styles in your context.

- Identify a major global social change within the last century and produce a ten page account of leadership processes in implementing this change.

COURSE DESCRIPTION

This course examines Social Change globally from both macro and micro perspectives; both long and short term. There are several dimensions including individual change, institutional change, social movements, and nonviolence, and eternal change.

COURSE OBJECTIVES

In completing this course the student will:

- Become familiar with diverse sociological perspectives of social change;

- Examine social change in Caribbean society from discovery to contemporary issues;

- Develop a greater understanding of institutional structures and contemporary issues;

- Improve writing ability, capacity for critical thinking, research, and analysis.

COURSE INSTRUCTION

The course objectives will be achieved through research, class discussions and activities, and written work. The instruction will incorporate various interactive exercises in which the student is expected to participate; designed to exemplify the topics under consideration.

COURSE TEXTS

Among texts named in the References are:

Moyer, Bill, JoAnn McAllister, Mary Lou Finley and Steve Soifer, (2001), *Doing democracy: The MAP Model for Organizing Social Movements*, New Society Publishers: Gabriola Island, British Columbia

Ritzer, George, (2000), *The McDonalization of Society*, New century ed., Pine Forge Press: Thousand Oaks, California

Zunes, Steven, Lester Kurtz, Sarah Beth Asher, (1991), eds., *Nonviolent Social Movements: A Geographical Perspective*, Blackwell: University of San Francisco

Students are required to read extensively beyond the References - see Resource Bibliography for suggested reading.

ASSESSMENT

Research project (25%) and presentation (10%)	35%
Mid term take home essay exam	20%
<u>Developmental</u> Readings entries (35 entries)	25%
Class participation & attendance	20%
TOTAL	100%

WRITTEN WORK

The written work for this class comprises developmental readings, a research essay, and a research project with presentation.

- Due dates: Please adhere to due dates of projects. The research project with presentation is a 120 day assignment with presentation at next core. The student's enrolment for this program is agreement to adhere to these assignment due dates. Students must apply for extensions which the professor will consider individually as it merits. In EX-TREME cases where late work may be deemed acceptable there will be downgrading to the assessment – see below for policies for each type of written work

- Submission: All assignments will be submitted online. Please keep copies of assignments readily available for presentation and copies for peers when presenting.

- Questions: Clarification and or other questions on assignments will be directed to lecturer of course with sufficient time ahead of due date. The lecturer may direct students into further research for the purpose of self-discovery.

- Unless otherwise specified, all assignments must be in complete sentence form (including developmental readings). Students are expected to present at a graduate level with appropriate and effective use of the English language. Those who have difficulty with writing are encouraged to seek assistance for improvement in writing. In students' extensive reading and research, in addition to content, please attend to academic style, preciseness of use of language, and clarity.

- Sources: For the essay and research project only: at least two sources should be used to explore the topic/question outside of the textbooks. Sources for ALL ideas presented and quotations used are to be properly referenced using a recognized bibliographic format.

- Penalties will result if this referencing is not undertaken, amounting to a minimum of 10% of the grade. If students wish to include an anecdotal personal story, it is still to be written in third person. If students wish to include personal ideas, seek at least two sources for this idea in order to prove its validity, or demonstrate how this idea is derived from two other sources.

Remember: Don't confuse your own subjective interpretation with sociological ones and avoid value statements in substitution for critical thinking.

RESEARCH PROJECT – 35%

- *25 % Written component:* Details of project will be assigned during week of classes.

- *10% Presentation component:* an oral presentation is required by all students. Presentations will be at following core.

RESEARCH ESSAY – 20%

Details of requirements were previously distributed.

DEVELOPMENTAL READINGS – 25%

There will be 35 entries. An insight should be provided for each entry. These entries are an opportunity for students to explore feelings and thoughts about various issues discussed in class and in the textbook, without having to provide academic argument. However, thoughts are to be elucidated. Assessment of entries focuses on use of English, comprehensiveness and appropriateness of entries, depth in uncovering and exploring reasons for personal/individual thoughts and feelings. Entries should include students' attitudes, behaviors and FEELINGS about topics, not simply a cognitive analysis. Analysis of entries will not be graded as right or wrong; these are simply expressions of opinions, feelings, and attitudes. Analysis and expressions must convey an understanding and application of the entry.

PARTICIPATION – 10%

Informed and constructive participation in class discussion is expected. The course outline requires extensive readings for informed participation. Please read and/or prepare all materials prior to class period for which they are assigned. It is also helpful if students approach this class with an open mind and a sense of enthusiasm for learning. Participation is awarded for involvement in in-class activities, exercises, discussions, and so on. Please note that participation points are awarded based on *active involvement* and *genuine participation.*

ATTENDANCE – 10%

Attendance is expected and will be taken during each class session. OASIS' Student's Handbook describes methodologies and gives explanation for brevity of class time. This is a doctoral program and students must recognize the significant responsibility and accountability each person bears. Additionally, general academic policies of OASIS *require* complete attendance and active participation in class. Attendance and participation are *important* to a student's learning and that of other students in this class. It will become apparent if a student has not completed the readings and thus is unable to contribute in constructive discussion.

Attendance to four classes is imperative. Any student who misses a class will repeat course at next offering. If a student is unable to attend all classes, then it is advisable that he/she withdraws from the course or else risk the application of penalties in the assessment. Four class periods during one week dedicated for attendance should not be misappropriated. The lecturer understands there are unexpected circumstances. Please weigh choices carefully before subordinating a class period in favor of another responsibility. Should a student miss one class under reasonable circumstances a discussion between professor and student will attempt to determine a method to compensate for this gap in learning.

Punctuality is an excellent habit to develop. Absolutely! Let all involved demand high standards of each other. A student should call ahead of time if there is an emergency.

GRADING SCALE

A	90	- 100% - Far Exceeds Expectation
B	80	89% - Exceeds Expectation
C	70	79% - Meets Expectations
D	60	69% - Fails to Meet Expectations
F		59% and below – Redo Assignment

Alternatively:

A = Honor grade; indicates comprehensive mastery of required work.

B = Indicates high level of performance in meeting course requirements.

C = Indicates satisfactory level of performance.

D = Indicates lowest passing grade.

F = Indicates significant additional effort required.

An "A" denotes exceptional work. All assignments and policies indicated above and below must be completed and/or carried out in a satisfactory manner in order to receive a passing grade in this class.

A student at doctoral level is a potential specialist in each subject area covered based on extensive research completed. This is subject to interpretation. Students have choice between dual motivations. Does that student perform to meet external expectations of his professor or school or does he maintain personal standards far exceeding external expectations? Students bear responsibility to cause their learning to be worthwhile. Effort is required.

Assignments are loaded and graded online. Students should retain copies of all assignments should the School require resending of assignment. Students should pay attention to comments of lecturer on graded work which may be useful in future assignments.

STUDENT RIGHTS AND RESPONSIBILITIES
for Social Change and Leadership

A classroom allows for conversation among all. In aggregate students bring more to the classroom than a professor. There should be an atmosphere of mutual respect by all concerned. OASIS and this professor recognize rights, responsibilities, and knowledge of students. Following is a list of mutual expectations for this course. These can be discussed and adjusted before or during core.

Your rights:

- Essential theories of leadership and Social Change will be highlighted and discussed during class

- A clear explanation of written work including assessment

- Respect

- Students can make appointments during core with lecturer

- The lecturer may provide reasonable assistance individually in understanding the course material if necessary

- Both students and lecturer should input into course topics to be discussed

Your responsibilities:

- Your education

- Punctuality

- Attend all classes

- Hand in all assignments on time

- Do readings prior to class

- Contribute to class discussions and activities

- Respect for all including self

- Seek explanations and help if needed

- If having learning challenges or other issues which will affect your learning, inform me in advance

- Know what is taking place each class with regard to readings and assignment of written work and due dates

- Turn off any cell phones or pagers

As your professor, I am responsible for facilitating learning and serving as a resource for you in this class. It is my job to challenge you, to consider your work against the standards I set forth, and to evaluate your efforts based on my experience, formal learning, and teaching. As students, you are responsible for being here, participating in class, completing assignments in an appropriate and timely fashion, and for learning. Staying on top of things, being self-motivated, and putting forth adequate effort are all a part of the equation for you to earn a good grade in this course.

That said, I'd like to remind you that it is best if you do not equate your self worth with your grade in this class or on any assignment. You may be an "A+ person" who happened to perform at a C+ level on a given assignment. Remember that grades are an indication of your performance in mastering the material at hand at one point in time. They do not condemn you to a life of doom and drudgery. Nor are they an indicator of your professor's views of you as a person. Reflect on your grade in an honest and realistic fashion before reacting. Remember that I am here to offer constructive criticism of your speeches, papers, and so on. Digest that criticism and then ask yourself questions like: *Did I put in the preparation time that would've been necessary to receive a better grade?, Did I understand the assignment as fully as I could have?, Did I turn in all the required paperwork?, Did I do an adequate job of proofreading, running a spell check?* If you find that you still have questions about how you can improve or about course content, come see me and we will talk about additional ways for you to work on your mastery of the subject matter.

A few thoughts about attitude... It has been my experience that students who approach their education with a sense of excitement and a willingness to learn are more productive students. Holding on to the belief that you HAVE TO take this course prevents you from embracing the point of view that you GET TO take this course. This course may be outside your major area of interest, but the content will still relate to your daily activities at home, work, profession, and school. We will laugh, we will experience nervousness, we will think critically, we will speak, we will listen, and we will learn. Most importantly, we will do these things *together*. There is *no* room for negative criticism of others and there is *no* room for laughter at the expense of another in this class. Enjoy the class and look for the concepts to be applicable in your daily life and I think you'll be surprised at what you can accomplish this semester.

PLAGIARISM, ACADEMIC DISHONESTY, AND DISRUPTIVE BEHAVIOR

Cheating and plagiarism are unacceptable. *Plagiarism* is quoting from, paraphrasing, or using specific ideas contained in any published work, e.g. books periodicals, public documents, internet, etc…, or using another person's ideas without providing an appropriate citation or recognition which credits the author and/or origin of the work or idea, and presenting them as if they are your own. *Academic dishonesty* can refer to a range of inappropriate and unethical behaviors including but not limited to cheating on exams, falsification of sources, and so on. As in other courses at the School, students in this class are expected to do their own work and conduct themselves in a fair, honest, and ethical manner. Those who plagiarize or engage in academic dishonesty of any kind may **minimally** expect to fail the assignment at hand and perhaps the entire course. In addition, instances of academic dishonesty and plagiarism may be dealt with through proper School channels for investigation and disciplinary action.

"Disruptive behavior" includes but is not limited to talking when someone else has the floor, insensitivity to others, destructive (rather than constructive) criticism of another, arriving late, sleeping/inattentiveness during class, belligerent or aggressive behavior, among others. These are unbecoming behaviors. You have a right to maintain your own opinions and to disagree with others, but you must do so in a fashion that is conducive to learning and does not take the form of a personal attack on others. Minimally, you are expected to treat your classmates and your professor in a respectful fashion and they will return the favor. *Any behavior that obstructs or disrupts the classroom teaching and learning environment will be addressed. Serious or repeated breaches in appropriate behavior may result in a reduction of your final grade in the course and may be referred to additional University authorities.*

NOTE: The instructor reserves the right to change the course syllabus. The students will be given sufficient advanced notice of any changes should they arise.

COURSE OUTLINE

Chapters denote readings to be completed prior to each week. It is imperative that you read the chapter before coming to class so that you will have a basic foundation of the topic in class discussions and activities.

The first part of the course will deal with social change in general, theory and applied, the second part will deal with nonviolent social movements in the West, and the third part will deal with social movements on an international level.

Class 1

- Introduction of students, professor and course
- Topic: Introduction to social change & its theories
- Presentation of Essays

Class 2

- Topic: Introduction to major global social change
- Cite examples of major changes and impact

Class 3

- Topic: Institutional changes in the Caribbean
- Individual challenges of social change

Class 4

Other Topics:

- Life, death, and the future
- "McDonaldization" of Society
- Introduction to social movements & nonviolence
- Nonviolent social movements & Introduction –
- Doing democracy
- Social movements in Europe
- Nonviolent social movements

- Social movements in Africa & the Middle East
- Nonviolent social movements
- Social movements in Asia
- Social movements in the Americas

Journals (Suggested)

Journal #1

Past/present/future social change in the Caribbean: Compare your life to that of your parents/grandparents, do an interview with someone from previous generation, and hypothesize what life might be like for your children/grandchildren. (if you don't have any of these groups of people in your life or will not have, then consider those surrounding you during the same generations). Comment in terms of material and nonmaterial/ideational aspects as covered in class.

Journal #2

How have you experienced McDonaldization in your life? By providing examples from your own life, comment upon various aspects considering different institutions (see book for what institutions Ritzer discusses - but also use your critical thinking skills and look at other institutions), and how each of the four principles have been evident in your daily experience.

Journal 3#

Violence and Nonviolence

Discuss your personal experiences of violence of the various types explored in class or situations you have directly been witness to. Focus particularly on ecological violence, structural violence & psychological violence rather than the physical violence.

From the material presented in class, explore the Nonviolence in your own life, i.e. what are your experiences of Nonviolence (not simply aspects that are not violent). What are your thoughts about it Nonviolence (negative/positive aspects, disadvantages/advantages). From these two discussions, do you essentially see the world as non-violent or as violent?

Journal #4

What does peace mean to you? What are representations of peace in your life? Explore the concept of peace at various levels from the individual to the global. Do you feel the institution of the military supports or hinders your beliefs about what peace means to you? Consider this in terms of the individuals who comprise the military as well as those individuals who make decisions which affect the military, i.e. from the soldier to the commander in chief of the military.

Journal #5

How have social movements affected your life? Comment on various social movements that have taken place over the past 200 years, and explore in detail how the social changes that occurred due to the work of these social movements has directly impacted your life.

From this exploration and from the discussions in class, how do you FEEL about social movements? (Do not simply provide a cognitive assessment) For you what are the advantages/disadvantages in terms of you as an individual.

Resource Bibliography
and Suggested Reading

Leadership

Antonakis, John and. Day, D. (2012). The Nature of Leadership. 2d ed. Thousand Oaks, CA: SAGE

Avolio, Bruce J. (1999). Full Leadership Development: Building the Vital Forces in Organizations. SAGE.

Beck, John D. W., (2003). The Leader's Window: Mastering the Four Styles of Leadership to Build High-Performing Teams.: Wiley.

Blanchard, K. and Cathy, S.T. (2002). The Generosity Factor. Grand Rapids: Zondervan.

Bliss, E. C. (1991). Getting Things Done: The ABC's of Time Management. New York: Bantam.

Bonstingl, J. (1992). Schools Of Quality: An Introduction to Total Quality Management in Education. Alexandria, VA: ASCD.

Buckingham, M. (2012). Leadership development in the age of the algorithm. Harvard

Caldwell, Cam, Rolf Dixon, Larry Floyd, Joe Chaudoin, (2011). Diagnosing and Changing Organizational Culture: Based on the Competing Values Framework. San Francisco: Jossey-Bass/John Wiley & Sons.

Cannillar, B., Finkelstein,S., Hambrick, D. (2008) Stratigic Leadership: Theory and Research. Oxford U Press.

Cathcart, J. (1998). The Acorn Principle: Know Yourself – Grow Yourself. New York: St. Martin's Press.

Conger, J. A. (1992). Learning to Lead: The Art of Transforming Managers into Leaders. San Francisco: Jossey-Bass.

Cross, R., and Thomas, R. (2009). Driving Results Through Social Networks: How Top Organizations Leverage Networks for Performance and Growth. New York: Jossey-Bass

Daniels, Aubrey., (2000). Bringing Out the Best In People: How to Apply the Astonishing Power of Positive Reinforcement. McGraw-Hill.

De Pree, M. (1992). Leadership Jazz. New York: Doubleday.

De Pree, Max, (1997). Leading Without Power: Finding Hope in Serving Community. Jossey-Bass.

Depree, Max. (1997). Leading Without Power: Finding Hope in Serving Community. Jossey-Bass Publishers.

Drucker, P. F. (1990). Managing the Non-Profit Organization. New York: Harper Collins Publishers, Inc.

Dubrin, Andrew J. 2007. Leadership: Research Findings, Practice, and Skills, (5th ed). Boston, MA:

Duncan, Roger Dean. (2012). Change-Friendly Leadership: How to Transform Good Intentions into Great Performance. Maxwell Stone Publishing/Midpoint Trade Books .New York.

Fairholm, Gilbert W., (1991) Values Leadership: Toward a New Philosophy of Leadership. New York: Praeger.

Filson, B. (1993). Defining Moment: Motivating People To Take Action. Massachusetts: Williamstown Publishing Company.

Fisher, J. C., & Cole, K. M. (1993). Leadership and Management of Volunteer Administrators. San Francisco: Jossey-Bass.

Gardner, J., (1990). On Leadership, The Free Press.

Gelatt, J. P. (1992). Managing Nonprofit Organizations in the 21st Century. Phoenix, AR:Oryx Press.

Green, Hollis L. (2007) Interpreting an Author's Words. Nashville: Global EdAdvancePRESS.

Green, Hollis L. (2010). Sympathetic Leadership Cybernetics. Nashville: GlobleEdAdvancePress.

Green, Hollis L. (2010). Transformational Leadership in Education. 2nd Edition. Nashville: Global EdAdvancePRESS.

Green, Hollis L. (2013) Remedial and Surrogate Parenting. Nashville: Global EdAdvancePRESS.

Green, Hollis L. (2018) The EVERGREEN Devotional New Testament. C.A.F.E. Edition. Nashville: Global EdAdvancePRESS.

Greenleaf, Robert K., (1998). The Power of Servant-Leadership: Essays. San Francisco: Berrett-Koehler Publishers.

Greenleaf, Robert K., (2002). Servant Leadership: a Journey Into the Nature of Legitimate Power and Greatness. Paulist Press.

Grove, J., Kibel, B., Haas, T. (2007) EvaluLEAD: An Open-Systems Perspective on Evaluating Leadership Development. Handbook of Leadership Development Evaluation. K. Hannum, J. Martineau, and C. Reinelt, Eds. San Francisco: Jossey-Bass.

Hackman, Michael Z., (1996). Leadership: a Communication Perspective. Prospect Heights, IL: Waveland Press..

Hersey, Paul, Kenneth H. Blanchard and Dewey Johnson. (2001). Management of Organizational Behavior: Utilizing Human Resources, 8th ed. Upper Saddle River, NJ: Prentice-Hall, Inc.

Hesselbein, F. and Johnston, R., editors (2002). A Leader to Leader Guide On High-Performance Organizations. New York: Jossey-Bass Inc.

Holman, B. and Holman L. (1999). Turning Dreams into Success. Lexington, KY: A Lessons in Leadership Publication.

Hughes, Richard L. (1998). The Leader's Companion: Insights on Leadership: Service, Stewardship, Spirit, and Servant-Leadership. Wiley. New York.

Jaffe, D. T., Scott, C. D. & Tobe, G. R. (1994). Rekindling Commitment: How to Revitalize Yourself, Your Work, and Your Organization. California: Jossey-Bass Inc., Publishers.

Jaworski, Joseph and Betty S. Flowers.(1998). Synchronicity: The Inner Path of Leadership. Berrett-Koehler Publishers.

Kotter, John. P. 1996. Leading Change. Boston, MA: Harvard Business School Press.

Kouzes, James M. and Barry Z. Posner. (2012). The Leadership Challenge, 5th Edition. San Francisco:

Krause, D. G. (1997). The Way of the Leader. New York: Berkley Publishing Company.

Lakey, B., Lakey, G., Napier, R., & Robinson, J (1995). Grassroots and Nonprofit Leadership: A Guide for Organizations in Changing Times. Pennsylvania: New Society Publishers.

LeMay, N. and Ellis, A. (2007). Evaluating Leadership Development and Organizational Performance.

Lynch, R. (1993). Lead! How Public and Nonprofit Managers Can Bring Out The Best in Themselves and Their Organizations. California: Jossey-Bass Publishers.

MacLeod, F. (1995). Forming and Managing a Non-Profit Organization in Canada. B.C., Canada: International Self-Counsel Press, Ltd.

Maxwell, J. C. (1995). Developing the Leaders Around You. Nashville: Thomas Nelson, Inc.

Maxwell, John C. (1998).The 21 Irrefutable Laws of Leadership: Follow Them and People Will Follow You. Thomas Nelson.

Maxwell, John C. 2006. The 360° Leader: Developing Your Influence from Anywhere in the Organization. Thomas Nelson Inc.

Mays, C. (1997). Anatomy of a Leader. Aurora, IL: Successories, Inc.

McAndrew, D.A. (2005). Literacy leadership: Six strategies for people work. Newark, DE: International Reading Association.

McLeish, B. J. (1995). Successful Marketing Strategies for Nonprofit Organizations. John Riley & Sons, Inc.

Morrison, E. K. (1994). Leadership Skills: Developing Volunteers for Organizational Success. Arizona: Fisher Books.

Nohria, N. and Khurana, R. (2010) Handbook of Leadership Theory and Practice. Harvard Press.

O'Brien, P. (1994). Positive Management: Assertiveness for Managers. San Diego: Pfeiffer and Company.

Pearson, Carol S. (Ed). 2012. The Transforming Leader: New Approaches to Leadership for the Twenty-First Century. Berret-Koehler Publishers, Inc.

Redding, J. C. & Catalanello, R. F. (1994). Strategic Readiness: The Making of the Learning Organization. Jossey-Bass Inc., Publishers.

Sandberg, Sheryl. (2013). Lean In: Women, Work, and the Will to Lead. New York: Knopf.

Scholtes, P. R. (1998). The Leader's Handbook. New York: McGraw Hill.

Senge, Peter M. (2006). The Fifth Discipline: The Art & Practice of the Learning Organization. New York: Doubleday.

Sosik, J.J. and Jung, D.I. 2010. Full range leadership development: pathways for people, profit, and Staff Managers. Greensboro, NC: Center for Creative Leadership.

Stanley, C. (1999). Success God's Way. Atlanta: In Touch Ministries.

Stern, G. J. (1990). Marketing Workbook for Nonprofit Organizations. Saint Paul, MN:Amherst H. Wilder Foundation.

Watts, D. (2003). Six Degrees: the science of a connected age. New York: W.W. Norton & Company

Wenger, E., McDermott, R., Snyder, W.M., (2002). Cultivating Communities of Practice. Cambridge, MA: Harvard Business School Press.

Wheatley, M. J. (1994). Leadership and the New Science: Learning about Organization from an Orderly Universe. San Francisco: Berret-Koehler Publishing Company.

Wren, J. T. (1995). The Leader's Companion. New York: The Free Press.

Young, D. R., Hollister, R. M., Hodgkinson, V. A. & Associates. (1993). Governing, Leading, and Managing Nonprofit Organizations. San Francisco: Jossey-Bass

Yukl, G. (2013). Leadership in Organizations. 8th ed. Upper Saddle River, NJ: Pearson.

Burke, M. A., & Liljenstolpe, C. (1992). Recruiting Volunteers: A Guide for Non-Social Change

Bakan, Joel (2004). The Corporation: The Pathological Pursuit of Profit and Power. New York: Simon and Schuster.

Bollier, David (2003). Silent Theft: The Private Plunder of Our Common Wealth (New York: Routledge.

Buckingham, M. (2007). Go: Put Your Strengths to Work. Free Press.

Bunker, B. B., Alban, B. T. (1997). The Handbook of Large Group Methods. San Francisco, CA: Jossey-Bass, Inc.

Camejo, Peter, Ed., (2005). SRI Advantage: Why Socially Responsible Investing Has Outperformed Financially; Gabriola Island, BC: New Society Publishers

Cooperrider, D., Sekerka, L. (2006). Toward a theory of positive organizational change. Organization Development: A Jossey-Bass Reader.

Cottor, R., Asher, A., Levin, J., Weiser, C. (2004). Experiential Learning Exercises In Social Construction: A Field Book for Creating Change. Taos Institute Publishing.

Green, Hollis L. (2013) Tear Down These Walls. Nashville: Global EdAdvancePRESS.

Johnson, S., Ludema, J. (1997). Partnering to build and measure organizational capacity: lessons from NGOs around the world. Grand Rapids, MI: Christian Reformed World Relief Committee (CRC).

Kegan, R., Lahey, L. L. (2002). How the Way We Talk Can Change the Way We Work. Jossey-Bass

Kotter, John P. (1996). Leading Change. Harvard Business School Press

Kretzmann, J. P., McKnight, J. L. (1993). Building communities from the inside out. Chicago, IL: ACTA Publications.

Laszlo, C. (2008). Sustainable Value: How the World's Leading Companies are Doing Well by Doing Good. Stanford University Press.

Piderit, S. K., Fry, R. E., Cooperrider, D. L. (2007). Handbook of transformative cooperation. Stanford University Press.

Quinn, R. E. (1996). Deep Change: Discovering the Leader Within. San Francisco, CA: Jossey-Bass Publishers.

Srivastva, S., Cooperrider, D. L. (Eds.). (1998). Organizational wisdom and executive courage (1 ed.). San Francisco, CA: The New Lexington Press.

Thatchenkery, T., Metzker, C. (2006). Appreciative Intelligence: Seeing the Mighty Oak in the Acorn. Berrett-Koehler Publishers.

Zenger, J. H., Folkman, J. (2002). The Extraordinary Leader: Turning Good Managers into Great Leaders. McGraw-Hill Trade.

Social Research

Babbie, Earl. (2001). The practice of social research (9th edition)

Belmont, CA: Wadsworth.

Bell, J. (1993). Doing your research project: a guide for first-time researchers in education and social science (2nd ed.). Buckingham;

Booth, V.(1993). Communicating in Science: Writing a Scientific Paper

Boston: Allyn and Bacon.

Bryman, Alan. (2008). Social Research Methods. Oxford University Press.

Buckingham, Alan and Peter Saunders. (2004). The survey methods

Buckingham; Philadelphia: Open University Press

De Vaus, David. (2001). Research design in social research. Thousand Oaks, CA: Sage

DeVaus, D.A. (1995). Surveys in social research (4th ed.). St. Leonards,

DeVellis R.F. (1991) Scale Development. Newbury Park, Sage

Franzosi, Roberto. (2008). Content Analysis. Sage.

Green, Hollis L. (2011) Designing Valid Research—A Brief Study of Research
    Methodology, Nashville: GlobalEAdvancePRESS.

Green, Hollis L.. (2014 PDF manuscript) Research Methods for Problem Solvers,
    Nashville: GlobalEd AdvancePRESS.

Hessler, R.M. (1992). Social research methods. St. Paul: West Pub. Co.

Homan R. (1991). The Ethics of Social Research, New York, NY,

Hugh L. Marsh.] New York : Quorum Books.

Hult, C.A. (1996). Researching and writing in the social sciences. interpreting
    behavioral data: An introduction to statistics. Pacific Grove, CA: Brooks/Cole
    Publishing Corporation.

Lewis-Beck, MS, ed. (1994) Basic Measurement. London, SAGE.

Pilcher, D.M. (1990). Data analysis for the helping professions: a

practical guide. Newbury Park, CA: Sage.

Punch, Keith.(2005) An Introduction to Social Research: quantitative quantitative
    approaches. Pearson, Allen and Bacon.

Reid. S. (1987). Working with statistics: an introduction to quantitative

research. London: University College London Press.

Salkind N.J.(2007) Statistics for People Who (Think They) Hate Statistics. Sage.

Singleton, Jr., R.A., Straits, B.C., & Straits, M.M. (1993). Approaches to

social research. New York: Oxford University Press.

Spoull, N.L. (1995). Handbook of research methods: a guide for students of psychology,
    education and the social sciences.

Elmsford, NY: Pergamon.

Swanson, G.A. and Green, Hollis L. (1992). Understanding Scientific Research: An
    Introductory Handbook for the Social Professions, Oxford/ACRSS Books.

Weinbach, R.W., & Grinnell, R.M. (1995). Statistics for social workers (3rd

Williams, M., & May, T. (1996). Introduction to the philosophy of social workbook:
    From design to analysis. Cambridge, UK: Polity Press.

Yates, Simeon J. (2004). Doing social science research. London, UK:

York: Continuum.

Strategic Management

Allison, Michael & Kaye, Jude. (1997). "Why Plan?" Strategic Planning for Nonprofit Organizations, New York: John Wiley & Sons.

Barker, J. A. (1992). The Future Edge: Discovering the New Paradigms of Success. NY: William Morrow and Company, Inc.

Drucker, P. (1995). Managing in a Time of Great Change. NY: Dutton.

Earley. J. (1997). Transforming Human Culture - Social Evolution and the Planetary Crises. Albany, NY: State University of New York Press.

Gharajedaghi, J. (1999). Systems Thinking: Managing Chaos and Complexity - A Platform for Designing Business Architecture. Woburn, MA: Butterworth-Heinemann.

Gill, S. (2000). The Manager's Pocket Guide to Organizational Learning. Amherst MA: HRD Press.

Haour, Georges, Mieville, Laurent, (2010). From Science to Business: How firms create value by partnering with universities. Palgrave Macmillan

Hay, Robert D. (1990) Strategic management in non-profit organizations, Westport: Greenwood Press.

Jensen, W. D. (2000). Simplicity: The New Competitive Advantage in a World of More, Better, Faster. NY: Perseus.

Maznevski, M., DiStefano, J., (2009). International Management Behavior: Leading with a Global Mindset. John Wiley & Sons.

Peiperi, M.; Jick, T., 3rd edition, (2011) Managing Change: Cases and concepts. McGraw-Hill,

Read, S., Sarasvathy, S., Dew, N., Wiltbank, R., Ohlsson, A-V. (2011) Effectual Entrepreneurship: What are you waiting for? Routledge,Swanson, G. A. and Miller,James Grier. (1989) Measurement and

Interpretation in Accounting: A Living Systems Theory Approach.   New York: Quirum Books.

Swanson, G.A. (1992). Management observation and communication theory. [with Heikki Heiskanen.] New York: Quorum Books.

Social Change

Bakan, Joel (2004). The Corporation: The Pathological Pursuit of Profit and Power. New York: Simon and Schuster.

Bollier, David (2003). Silent Theft: The Private Plunder of Our Common Wealth (New York: Routledge.

Buckingham, M. (2007). Go: Put Your Strengths to Work. Free Press.

Bunker, B. B., Alban, B. T. (1997). The Handbook of Large Group Methods. San Francisco, CA: Jossey-Bass, Inc.

Camejo, Peter, Ed., (2005). SRI Advantage: Why Socially Responsible Investing Has Outperformed Financially; Gabriola Island, BC: New Society Publishers

Cooperrider, D., Sekerka, L. (2006). Toward a theory of positive organizational change. Organization Development: A Jossey-Bass Reader.

Cottor, R., Asher, A., Levin, J., Weiser, C. (2004). Experiential Learning Exercises In Social Construction: A Field Book for Creating Change. Taos Institute Publishing.

Green, Hollis L. (2013) Tear Down These Walls. Nashville: Global EdAdvancePRESS.

Johnson, S., Ludema, J. (1997). Partnering to build and measure organizational capacity: lessons from NGOs around the world. Grand Rapids, MI: Christian Reformed World Relief Committee (CRC).

Kegan, R., Lahey, L. L. (2002). How the Way We Talk Can Change the Way We Work. Jossey-Bass

Kotter, John P. (1996). Leading Change. Harvard Business School Press

Kretzmann, J. P., McKnight, J. L. (1993). Building communities from the inside out. Chicago, IL: ACTA Publications.

Laszlo, C. (2008). Sustainable Value: How the World's Leading Companies are Doing Well by Doing Good. Stanford University Press.

Piderit, S. K., Fry, R. E., Cooperrider, D. L. (2007). Handbook of transformative cooperation. Stanford University Press.

Quinn, R. E. (1996). Deep Change: Discovering the Leader Within. San Francisco, CA: Jossey-Bass Publishers.

Ramjattan, S. (2012) God's Work Done God's Way. Nashville: Global EdAdvancePRESS.

Srivastva, S., Cooperrider, D. L. (Eds.). (1998). Organizational wisdom and executive courage (1 ed.). San Francisco, CA: The New Lexington Press.

Thatchenkery, T., Metzker, C. (2006). Appreciative Intelligence: Seeing the Mighty Oak in the Acorn. Berrett-Koehler Publishers.

Zenger, J. H., Folkman, J. (2002). The Extraordinary Leader: Turning Good Managers into Great Leaders. McGraw-Hill Trade.

www.ingramcontent.com/pod-product-compliance
Lightning Source LLC
Chambersburg PA
CBHW081229090426

42738CB00016B/3230